# Messiah
## WITHIN

# Messiah WITHIN

*A Guide to Embracing
Your Inner Divinity*

## ROBIN H. CLARE

INTRODUCTION BY JAMES F. TWYMAN,
NEW YORK TIMES BESTSELLING AUTHOR

**BALBOA**
PRESS
A DIVISION OF HAY HOUSE

Balboa Press books may be ordered through booksellers or by contacting:

Balboa Press
A Division of Hay House
1663 Liberty Drive
Bloomington, IN 47403
www.balboapress.com
1-(877) 407-4847

ISBN: 978-1-4525-4925-5 (sc)
ISBN: 978-1-4525-4926-2 (hc)
ISBN: 978-1-4525-4924-8 (e)

Library of Congress Control Number: 2012905275

Nancy Simonds – Copyeditor
Eduardo Barrios - Logo

Printed in the United States of America

Balboa Press rev. date: 04/24/2014

# Dedications:

To my mother, Mona for teaching me how to love unconditionally.
To Leslie, for listening to every story with love and compassion.
To Ori, Gaby, Garrett and Hailey for being my beautiful family.

# TABLE OF CONTENTS

# Acknowledgements

I have been blessed to have an outstanding Spiritual Support Team who has guided me on this extraordinary journey to finding my Messiah Within.

**Exceptional Teachers:** Yeshua ben Yosef, Sri AmmaBhagavan, Creatious (Cathy Fischer), Angelic Council and Healers of LIGHT (Pat Caffrey) and Sheryl Blumenthal (Messenger for the I AM & Council of Elders and my spiritual sister).

**Spiritual Guides and Loved Ones:** My gratitude for your perpetual Divine guidance is beyond words.

**JT:** Yeshua asked me, "Who would you like to be your writing coach?" I said "James Twyman, of course, I love his work." and you arrived to help. You have been an invaluable coach and friend.

**Nick Bunick:** Your deep knowing of Yeshua in *Time for Truth* inspired me greatly.

**Noteworthy Advisors:** Mona & Carl Back, Eduardo Barrios, Colleen Behan, Patricia Bonsignore, Ori Clare, David Cruz, Jatin Desai, Sheila Finkel-Boucher, Doreen Fishman, Bob Foley, Michael Jernegan, Wendy Kolanz, Leslie Korus, Sri Madhu, Fal Patel, Nancy Simonds, Abby Straus and Linda Tomb.

**Sacred Friends:** You continue to hold space for me to fulfill my Divine destiny and I am immensely grateful.

**Jatin, Fal and Anjali:** May all who enter The ATMA Center leave knowing Oneness.

**Spiritual Community Members:** I am delighted to share this path with each one of you.

**Eduardo:** Your generosity and creative vision is truly a gift to me.

**Ed (Blue Shutters Inn):** You do have the best job in the world!

**College Love:** I am glad that we had the chance to say sorry to each other.

**Twin Flame:** I will always cherish our sacred journey.

**Tyler Hill Family:** Our past, our present and our future under one roof – we are so blessed.

**Dad:** I feel your presence every day.

**Mona, Carl, Alan and Michael:** "Life is like a box of chocolates" and I love all the choices.

**Hailey:** Thank you for being my constant companion.

**Gaby and Garrett:** Thank you for choosing me to be your mom.

**And to my husband, Ori:** Thank you for agreeing to tell our love story.

# Introduction: James F. Twyman

## How often does God speak to you?

This may seem like a strange question at first, but lately it's been getting a lot of attention. When Neale Donald Walsch wrote his hugely successful series of books called "Conversations with God," many people, especially those who knew him, thought he had lost his mind. Who was he, a formerly homeless man whose life was in a shambles, to speak directly to the creator of the Universe? In the end, especially as people began reading, then sharing the amazing result of that exchange, the question began to shift. It was no longer who is Neale, or you for that matter, to have a conversation with God, but rather, who are you NOT to? Is it possible that God is always talking to us, even pushing us into direct communication, but we simply haven't been listening?

I've often thought that the biggest problem with God has nothing to do with God, but rather, our ideas of how we define the ultimate source of all that exists. Definitions get in the way, especially when we're trying to describe something that's impossible to rationalize. Before long we get into a battle of human wills—*my God is better than your God*, or *God is on my side but not on yours*. Wars have been fought for ideas like these since the beginning of human history, and even when it seems to be about something else, there's often a link back to the idea that I'm right about God and you're not. Most of all—*God loves me more than he (or she) loves you*.

Do you realize that more people have been killed in the name of Jesus than any other person in the history of the world? Wasn't he the same man who said to lay down your sword and love your enemy? Strange how we can turn things around so completely, making a mockery of someone whose only desire was to bring us back to God.

Speaking of Jesus, it's funny how often Christians forget that he wasn't a Christian at all. He was a Jew, completely committed to his people. For centuries Christians blamed the Jews for his death, making them responsible for killing the Son of God and forcing every generation thereafter to pay to the crime. I wonder what Jesus would have thought about that policy? The same man who made forgiveness the cornerstone of his philosophy would have surely had a different attitude than: "Kill them all, and let God sort out his own." Funny what we do . . . all in the name of the Divine.

But I digress. This is supposed to be an introduction to a book about a nice Jewish girl who talks to Jesus—setting things straight once and for all. I remember the first time I heard about Robin's project. I thought: "At last someone is writing a book about the esoteric teachings of Yeshua ben Yosef (that's his real name, in case you were wondering), intended for the Jewish people he loved." She shared many of the stories she's included here during a series of coaching sessions that I had with her to help her refine the book you're about to read. I loved it—especially the ways she struggled with the material, and how it must have felt to live in a very Jewish community, with a husband studying to be a rabbi, all the while talking to the one guy nice Jewish girls are never supposed to mention.

It's that kind of struggle that makes a book like this great, and I think she accomplished that task. It's personal and universal at the same time. It makes us think about who we are, and our responsibility to the world in general. This, after all, is what the message of Yeshua is all about. He didn't come to force us further apart, but to show us what we can be when we lay aside our differences and focus on how we are the same.

I feel very connected to this beautiful book, not only because I've been watching its careful progression for over a year now, but because

I think the time is right for a message of such clarity. Going back to the original question I posed, God speaks to you every moment of your life. Robin was just brave enough to listen and write down what she heard.

Now the question is: Will you do the same?

# PART I

# Introduction

My husband is a religious, Conservative Jew. Imagine his expression when I told him that I had just had a conversation with a man that no "real" Jew would admit to having any kind of personal relationship with: Jesus. The look on his face said it all; he thought I had *finally* gone off the "deep end." To make matters worse, neither one of us was very comfortable with what Jesus had asked of me.

Yeshua ben Yosef had been trying to get my attention for ten years. Yeshua is the Aramaic name of Jesus, and was how he was called during his lifetime as a Jew. As was the custom to include one's patrilineage in one's name, "ben Yosef" means "son of Joseph". He was considered a Jewish teacher.

For most of the ten years, my communication with Yeshua has been through the vehicle of channeling. Channeling is an ancient form of communication whereby information from the spiritual realm is shared with human beings through a gifted person otherwise known as a channel. In my case, over the course of many channeled readings and guided messages, I would consistently be informed that Yeshua ben Yosef was my main spiritual guide. How could that be? How could this Jewish woman be guided by Yeshua or Jesus Christ as he is more commonly referred to? Why was he choosing me?

## My Inner Conflict

Of all the great Ascended Masters, Yeshua was the last one with whom I would ever have wanted to connect on a spiritual basis and, therefore, I was doing my best to ignore his attempts to connect with me. The plain and simple truth was that I was scared of him. I could not even look at a picture of him without looking away. I was deeply attached to the generational fears of the Jewish people, after 2000 years of persecution for being wrongly accused of killing Jesus. Imagine my inner conflict: I was afraid of Yeshua and yet I felt compelled to walk in his footsteps

Why had Yeshua entered my life? Where were the parallels? We were both Jewish. We both had to look beyond the cultural norms and expectations of our religious communities to speak our truth. We both deeply believed in the concept of Oneness: that there is no separation between God and us. God and we are One.

The concept of Oneness begins as an intellectual concept—one that we might read about in a book such as this. But then, as one begins to discover one's own inner divinity, we recognize that Oneness is not a concept but an experience. It becomes part of who you are at your core—and it is the ultimate gift from God.

Yet my perceived fear of Yeshua created a sense of separation between us. Therefore, before I could reach my knowing of Oneness with the Divine, I first had to reach a state of Oneness with Yeshua. "How do I reach a state of Oneness with Yeshua—the being I most fear?" I thought to myself. I began with what I knew we had in common, a deep belief that we are One with the Divine. While I had a strong *belief*, I knew that I had to reach a state of *knowing*, like Yeshua had.

## My Path of Oneness

In my spiritual studies, I have read many books on Yeshua's teachings as a rabbi before the formation of Christianity. I discovered that Yeshua was the ultimate teacher of Oneness. As he travelled the Holy Land, he spoke and taught about reaching a state of Oneness with the Divine. Yeshua was able to reach beyond the teachings of the Torah to become One with God. He knew and expressed that the "Kingdom of God lies Within." He was not hampered by long-standing interpretations of the Torah—he knew what he knew and he was not afraid to say it. Through esoteric meditation techniques shared with him by John the Baptist (also a Jew), he discovered a conduit for his great healing abilities and his teaching of Oneness.

Everywhere I turned the teachings of Yeshua and my path would intersect, because his teachings and my knowing were truly one and the same. But the Jewish person in me had a hard time with the term "Christ Consciousness" (the "new age" teachings of Yeshua) until I understood the meaning of "Christ" (as the Anglicized version of the original Greek word for "anointed one") in its simplest interpretation: "the embodiment of God in form." In essence, it would be as appropriate to call my guide Yeshua Christos, or simply Yeshua, as it would be to call him Jesus Christ.

## A Nice Jewish Girl

Here I was this nice Jewish girl studying the teachings of Yeshua and totally relating to them. I just could not understand why his teachings resonated so deeply with me. To some this may sound kind of silly, but Jewish people are not comfortable talking about "Christ" and typically do not discuss the teachings of Yeshua ben Yosef either. It's a taboo subject and I knew that I had to have a lot of *chutzpah* (Yiddish for "nerve") to write this book. We live in a town that is 40% Jewish. It was a great place demographically and spiritually to begin my journey and to honor Yeshua's Request, but also may turn out to be a challenging place to expose my true life's purpose.

A good example of what I thought I would be up against happened in my private healing practice. In this capacity, I serve as a conduit to the spiritual realm through reading the Akashic Records. A Chassidic Jewish man came for a session. In our session, Yeshua asked me to share a series of messages with this client. Needless to say, the client was shocked that Yeshua had come into the session but he listened peacefully to the messages received. The next day I was shopping in our kosher supermarket preparing for Shabbat and my client came in with his rabbi. He said, "Rabbi—I would like you to meet my meditation teacher". We greeted each other cordially and then the client said, "And she talks to Jesus!" The Rabbi said, "Oy, Robin, that's not so good." I responded, "It's really not so bad, would you like to chat more about it?" The subsequent conversation did not occur.

## Becoming Spiritually Guided

What I discovered in the process of writing this book is that my path of Oneness had been divinely orchestrated by Yeshua. I became aware of and deeply connected to a team of energetic and human beings comprised of angels, spiritual guides, deceased loved ones and my cherished earthly spiritual teachers (my Earth angels). I lovingly refer to them all as my Spiritual Support Team.

In retrospect, I understood how each step on the journey was timed perfectly; within the parameters of how prepared I was to hear each teaching, to do the emotional, spiritual and physical healing required, and to grow further in my spiritual development. At times, Yeshua and my Spiritual Support Team would spoon-feed the information to me with humorous moments of wisdom and with cheerful connections to other people on my path. At other times, they would knock me over the head with a "spiritual 2 x 4" because the lesson they wanted to impart was bigger, more personal and profoundly more important.

Through a series of four messages I received in 2010, I began to gain greater clarity about my relationship to Yeshua, including why he became my spiritual guide, the purpose of our ten-year journey and, of course, The Request. Each of the four messages built upon the previous one in scope and importance.

# MESSAGES FROM YESHUA

## Yeshua's First Message

The first message I received from Yeshua came while I was in a deep meditative state. He said to me, ***"When will you accept that I was a Jew, Robin, and that my teachings were based in my deep love for Judaism?"*** Like the majority of the educated world, I knew *Yeshua was a Jew,* but that's where we seem to leave it—Yeshua was a Jew. We generally do not go further to explore his life within the context of religious isolation vs. pursuit of world peace and living in a state of Oneness. What if we could find the connections with Yeshua's teachings for all religious groups within his teachings of universal Oneness? Would this remove the veil of separation? I know that it was in my <u>acceptance</u> of Yeshua as a Jew, that I was able to connect with him and gain greater clarity about my own path.

## Yeshua's Second Message

The second message came in a channeled session. Yeshua said to me, ***"The key to reaching a state of Oneness and to the acceptance of my teachings is for everyone to forget that I was a <u>man</u>. It is in our view of me as a man that our problems begin. I was neither a Jewish man nor a Christian man, but I was an energetic being in complete Oneness with the Divine (or God). Therefore, my Request to you will not be about my teachings as a Jewish rabbi or my teachings as a beloved Christian master, but about an all knowing consciousness, the ultimate sense of Oneness with All That Is."***

On the surface, the second message seemed to contradict the first one. But I came to see it was just an expansion of the first message to develop a more universal acceptance of Yeshua's role during his mortal lifetime.

## Yeshua's Third Message

During this period, Yeshua guided me to read a series of books and articles, all with the same theme: *"As the Chosen People, the Jews can choose World Peace."* In each of the writings, the meaning was clear: If the Jewish people can remove the energy of persecution from our cultural identity and shift to a consciousness of Oneness, then there will be peace in the Middle East and, ultimately, the whole world. That was quite a message to receive. Could Yeshua be sharing this message with others around the globe at the same time?

A light bulb went on in my head. If the Jewish people "chose" to accept the teachings of Yeshua ben Yosef or the global teachings of Oneness, we would take a huge step towards world peace. We are talking here about global Oneness, about accepting our enemies as part of the Oneness. The Jewish people have a deeply rooted preoccupation with our sense of persecution because, quite frankly, it's true. In every generation over the last 3000 years, groups of people have been "out to get us."

In the teachings of Abraham-Hicks and the Law of Attraction, we learn that our thoughts become our beliefs. Throughout the history of the Jewish people, we have faced constant and relentless persecution. But, do we keep anticipating that this will happen? Are we manifesting this outcome in the universal mind of the Jewish people? Conversely, can we "choose" a new outcome? If we "choose" to accept that we are *all* One with the Divine—not just Jews, but our enemies too—would that shift the energy of our religious persecution energy to one of peaceful co-existence? Can we simply "choose" to materialize world peace?

In the fall of 2010, I was immersed in the messages from Yeshua, but, to be honest, I was still conflicted over being a Jewish woman guided by Yeshua. I knew that finding peace from this conflict was the next step in my journey. I arranged a private healing session with one of my Oneness teachers. We called in Yeshua to join us in a deep meditation. Yeshua then showed me my past life as a Jewish person in the Holocaust. In that lifetime, I chose to "hide and deny" my association with my Jewish identity. I now know that the energy of shame I felt then at having to take this tact is the energy I brought forth into this lifetime.

## The Divine Messenger's Request—
## Yeshua's Fourth Message

I then saw that the energy of shame from that lifetime directly corresponded to the energy of shame that I was feeling about being spiritually guided by Yeshua in this lifetime. While I chose to deny my Jewish identity in that lifetime, I was now feeling the shame of being perceived as a "Jew for Jesus". This phase is used to describe the Messianic Jews and others, who think that Yeshua or Jesus is the Jewish Messiah. While I acknowledge their perspective, the Yeshua that I have come to know is simply a Divine Messenger of God with the following extraordinary message for mankind.

Yeshua energetically expanded my heart for me to hear the fourth message and, finally, The Request. In a beautiful meditative state, Yeshua shared with me the following: *"We are in a time of great shift for mankind and this shift will enable each person to find God Within. We do not need to be looking for the Messiah in an outside source; the Messiah resides within each of us. My Request of you is to write a book called* **Messiah Within**, *a multi-cultural book on how each person can find the Messiah Within his or her self or find his or her own Oneness with the Divine. If each person on Earth, including the Jews, could find the Messiah Within his or her self,* *then there would be no conflict because we would all be One. This revelation could bring about a lasting world peace."*

## Messiah Consciousness

Yeshua stressed that it was particularly important for me to tell this story from the perspective of my Judaic roots. Now I was being asked to write a book and to share my closely kept secret (my relationship with Yeshua) with the Jewish community and the world. The combination of the two requests was daunting and would take courage for me to open to a new dimension in my life.

I would have to ask myself this question: Are we blessed to understand and live the teachings of Yeshua ben Yosef or do we continue to allow cultural norms to prevent us from shifting to possibly the greatest knowing in our lives? Yes, Yeshua brought a messianic message but he was <u>not</u> The Messiah. His message to me clearly stated that we all have the potential to be our own Messiah. Once this knowing becomes part of the preeminent consciousness of our planet, we can then say that we have entered the Messianic Age or that the Messiah has truly arrived. For, you see, the Messiah is not one being, it is all of us living in our most conscious state of global, shared awareness. Are we willing to expand our global awareness to include a multi-cultural perspective called the Messiah Consciousness? And that, regardless of one's religious path or spiritual inclination, we share a knowing that the Messianic Age is one where we will achieve our greatest connection to our most Divine state?

## The Conduit for Yeshua

Until now, the conversations with Yeshua have been one-sided, with him talking to me. I requested a two-way conversation with Yeshua—Jew to Jew—and I present our discussions in this book. I explored many topics with Yeshua, from why it is so important that world peace come through the Jews, to what happened 2000 years ago in his life and death as a Jew, to what is happening today in the world and how we can live our lives today in Oneness with God. I am not an expert on traditional religion or spirituality, I'm just an everyday person blessed to live with an extraordinary knowing. From this place, I agreed to be the conduit for the teachings of Yeshua ben Yosef to flow through to this book. Within the following pages, I will also share much more about the path that Yeshua had me take to finding my knowing of my own inner divinity, along with a process to follow so you can discover your own Messiah Within. See you on the path!

# A LETTER FROM YESHUA TO THE JEWISH COMMUNITY

## (AS CHANNELED THROUGH ROBIN)

Dearest Jewish Community:

What you will read in this book are the teachings that I learned in my life as a Jewish teacher and the result of a request to a modern day Spiritual Messenger, Robin, to share my story. This book presents multiple levels of stories—my lifetime as a Jew, Robin's path to finding her Messiah Within and my request of mankind to come together in Oneness during this time of great shift and change on our planet. In these channeled writings, I will refer to myself as "I" and I will also refer to myself as "We."

When I refer to myself as "We", I am referring to the collective energy of All Being, which each of us is a part of and all of. The world has changed dramatically since I walked the Earth. But in all the ways that truly count, not so much. Yes, we have seen amazing enhancements in technology and science, we have travelled to the moon and lands have been discovered that my contemporaries and I did not even know were on the Earth plane. But all of this advancement has created a world where man does not truly care about the other inhabitants of the Earth.

It may not be as bad as it sounds. Let me rephrase that . . . it looks a lot worse than it is because your world still lives in a state where power and money-mongers get the most attention by your media and by the general public. Fear sells. Therefore, your entertainment/

news industry shares information that most often scares people and makes them believe that the world is going to hell "in a hand-basket". The bottom line is that where this world goes is up to the collective energy of the planet—plain and simple. If you were to take your attention away from the negative and focus on the positive aspects of your beautiful lives, then the Universal energies would respond with greater opportunities for love to dominate the planet. But you choose to listen to the news, to allow your corporations to make excessive profits by exploiting the weak and the sick and to allow power hungry people to control your governments and your destiny. It takes a major catastrophe for you to care about each other. We are at least grateful that you still have magnificent compassion for each other when the chips are down.

But how do you live this life every day of your life? That, my friends, is the purpose of this book. By following the example set by Robin on her path, you will discover your path to your inner divinity and then into a state of Oneness with your family and friends, your community and then the world. Why am I directing this book towards the Jews? There are a few simple answers. First, I was a Jew, Robin is a Jew and, well, it is easiest to write to your people. But here is the main reason: for two years, I kept whispering in Robin's ear, "As the Chosen People, the Jews can choose World Peace." What does that mean, you might ask? I'll explain as we go.

The greatest enemy to mankind today is fear. The enemy is definitely not each other. Mankind has, for the first time, a unique opportunity to come into a state of unification. The Jewish people have been living in fear of persecution for the past 3000 years. This persecution complex is not individual-by-individual, but it is systemic amongst all Jews. And why not? It's been a very real problem. As a people, the Jews have maintained a connection to God that their enemies have not been able to maintain. The non-Jews' separation from God has created jealousy, fear and a desire to control the Jewish people in order to feel validated for their beliefs.

This is why I approached Robin to approach the Jews. God chose the Jews to receive the Torah at Mt. Sinai because *the Jews chose God.* Now, HaShem (the Kabalistic name of God) is asking that the Jews put down their shields and place down their swords first, in the name of Oneness with All Being. We are asking the Jews to stop being afraid of being persecuted.

As the Jews chose God first, we are asking the Jews to choose all of mankind and the Earth in Oneness. The Torah contains the *Mitzvot (*or commandments) that God requires in order to live in Oneness with mankind on the Earth plane. God made man/woman in His image for this sacred purpose. We recognize that this is an enormous request, because why would you put down your shield and sword when your enemies live right next door to you? But think about this: if the magnificent God-realized energy of the Jewish people were directed towards the unification of mankind rather than the defense of its own existence, the entire world's consciousness would raise dramatically. The Jewish people would no longer be afraid, their enemies would have no one to persecute and they, too, could get focused on the task of bringing Heaven to Earth through their religious or spiritual vehicles.

The answers provided by me in this book are intended to unite us and not divide us further. While you may have a completely different perspective, I honor you for that. We ask that you read this book with an open mind, for you will find that no matter what perspective you come from, the core teachings are the Light. From my original disciples of 2000 years ago to the current teachers of the Messiah Consciousness, the intention was always the same: to shine the light on our own shared divinity.

With deepest love,
Yeshua ben Yosef

# PART II

# First Conversation

**Robin:** Hello Yeshua. It is an honor to speak to you.

*Yeshua: Hello Robin. It is an honor to speak to you as well. Thank you for agreeing to do this book.*

**Robin:** You are most welcome. At times, the preparation and the writing of this book almost unraveled my life but I understood that this was my destiny. The experience of living this book at the same time I have been writing it has given me an extraordinary perspective on how the Universe works. I am deeply blessed to have known you on this level. May we accomplish what you first asked of me and that is for the Jewish people to honor your teachings, which were deeply rooted in Judaism, and that they come to desire the same outcome that we both share: Oneness with All Being.

**Robin:** Yeshua, why did you choose me to write this book?

*Yeshua: I did not choose you, Robin, you chose me or more importantly, you chose God. Throughout your many lifetimes you have always been connected to HaShem (God) in a way that gave you a deep sense of security even in the lifetimes that seemed hard. In this lifetime, the foundation provided by your family and friends has uncovered within you the courage to stand in your own knowing, a knowing that has been building over many lifetimes. And now, you stand firmly grounded and ready to share what you have known for millennia.*

**Robin:** I feel like I have known you forever, but how can that be so?

*Yeshua: In a way, you have known me for what may feel like forever, because you have shared the same knowing with me ever since you heard me speak 2000 years ago. Even in lifetimes where you were not free to speak your truth or where you were punished for speaking your truth, the knowing was always the same. Even at those times when your religious or cultural beliefs contradicted the teachings of Oneness, my original teachings made such a huge impact on you that they were carried forward in your soul's path or your DNA structure. Now we meet again and we can work together towards a greater world understanding.*

**Robin:** Yeshua, in two separate guided messages I received, both messages said that this book, *Messiah Within* was "essential." Can you share what that means?

*Yeshua: The intention of this book is to effect a shift in mankind from many perspectives, the first being that the Divine does not live outside oneself and that the fastest path to finding God is to look inside oneself. The second is to eliminate the sense of separation that exists between all peoples and especially between the Jewish people and the rest of mankind. The Jews chose God, not vice versa. This nuance is very, very important. Because the Jews chose God, he knew that he could rely on their commitment to protect the sacred teachings in the Torah. That no matter what strife they encountered, they would regard preservation of the Torah as paramount. Even if there was only one Jew left in the world, God knows that one solitary Jew would protect the Torah. At this critical juncture in time, God requires the people who chose God to also choose Oneness with all Mankind—as must all other groups of human beings on the planet today.*

**Robin:** In essence, by finding your Messiah Within, you become part of a global energy called the Messiah Consciousness, the veil of separation is removed and we can achieve Oneness with all Mankind. If only it were that simple! But we need to start somewhere and I know that you have a plan in mind.

*Yeshua: Yes, I do! The following twelve steps to becoming your Messiah Within are for all of mankind, not just the Jewish people. In the chapters to follow, you will read about Robin's journey to her Messiah Within, of the interesting experiences and people she met along the route.*

*Many of you will first recognize that there is another twelve step program that assists mankind in moving out of an addictive state. The completion of the first twelve step program may be necessary in order to proceed to this next step program.*

*For the twelve steps to becoming your Messiah Within, many of you will recognize these steps as ones that you have already taken in your own life. That is perfect and all that is required is that you finish the journey.*

*For those of you, who are new on the journey, continue to read the book and see how we (your Spiritual Support Team) provide you with abundant opportunities to achieve, step by step, your greatest knowing, your Messiah Within.*

# Yeshua's Path to Becoming Your Messiah Within

1. From your deepest point of stillness, find your inner voice that is whispering, "You are One with All."
2. Identify the spiritual path that is in greatest resonance with your inner knowing.
3. Become your Authentic Self.
4. Allow the Universe to provide you with what you need for your growth, alignment and well-being.
5. Heal your relationships with your immediate family.
6. Live your life fully without the fear of death.
7. Allow your Spiritual Support Team to lead the way.
8. Be open to learning all lessons placed on your path.
9. Return your heart to a state of emotional and energetic wholeness.
10. Live your life in the present moment without regret of the past or fear of the future.
11. Love deeply, unconditionally and without the chains of emotional bondage.
12. Know (not just think, feel or believe) that you are in complete Oneness with All Being.

**Robin:** Thank you, Yeshua. Shalom for now!

# *Step One*

*From your deepest point of stillness, find your inner voice that is whispering, "You are One with All"*

When I sat down to write this chapter, I asked Yeshua, "How do I tell the world about the spiritual journey that you guided me on to becoming my Messiah Within and what your desires are for the Jewish people and all of mankind during this time of great shift and change? Where do I start?" He responded, "At the beginning."

Sometimes the beginning seems like such a long time ago. But in reality, my process began ten *very* short years ago. I was just like many of you. I was caught up in a corporate career that paid me well and provided significant benefits for my family. My family and I lived what might be referred to as "The American Dream." But I always knew that I was being pulled towards something greater.

Ten years ago, for almost a year, I stood out on my deck every night and asked, "How can I be of the greatest service to Mankind?" While I never received a direct verbal answer, I knew there was someone listening to me, an energy that was not in physical form. Little did I know at the time that it was Yeshua, who would accompany me on a spiritual journey that would take me back to past lives and then all the way forward to visions of what the future holds for my life. What I can now say for sure is that when we truly know that we are spiritual beings having an earthly experience (as human beings), our lives are never again the same. This is my story and I hope it will give you strength to unveil your own.

The pages of books and the movie screens are filled with countless love stories about the love between a man and a woman, the love of parent for a child, the love of a child and his pet. We will soon discover that the greatest love story ever told is the one between ourselves and our own divinity. This book is the story of my greatest love—my path to finding my Messiah Within. For in this awakening of my heart, I have discovered that life is incredibly simple. In the teachings of Abraham-Hicks, we learn that we come into this world to experience contrast and we seek to align ourselves with a vibration that feels good. For once we align with the abundant positive energy of the Universe; our lives begin to go with the flow.

For many years, I knew all the right words but I did not align my vibration to match what I truly wanted. I remember once in a channeled reading, my spiritual guidance said to me, "For someone who knows so much about the Law of Attraction, you really suck at it." And, at the time, that was incredibly true. In retrospect, I could not align my Being with the Universe because I was not ready to live what I lovingly call the Messiah Within. It required a **process** to get here, an intense, deep process of learning about myself, my relationships and my connection to the Divine.

Carole King's classic song "Only Love is Real" has two *great* lines: *only love is real* and *everything else an illusion.* These two lines are also the teachings of the Great Masters and of the Divine. When we attune to this masterful inner knowing, life takes on a different meaning. This knowing first comes to us on an **intellectual** level, then we must transition to a **belief** that it is true, and finally, if we are blessed, we arrive at **knowing** that it is true. With the knowing that only love is real, we can accept others without judgment, we can forgive, we can love unconditionally . . . we can live in Oneness. We, in turn, become our Messiah Within and we are able to share this with others and live a life of peace, based in service.

This all sounds so lovely and simple, doesn't it? And yet, it is the hardest work we will ever do. For eternity, from everyday people to the Great Masters, all of humanity has struggled with loving itself, with seeing the Divine within. In my years of spiritual studies, I found that I have only been able to understand a complex spiritual concept when I arrive at the simplicity of its true meaning. I have discovered that this only happens when I stop thinking about it with my mind and focus on its true meaning with my heart.

Instinctively, I knew that I had in this and many other lifetimes muddied up the path to my Messiah Within. But now, I had to decide if I was going to be one of the brave ones, ready to look at "all my stuff," to attain what all of the Great Masters have promised: peace and serenity. My current life path was filled with the teachings of Great Masters past and present, from Yeshua ben Yosef to Sri AmmaBhagavhan. Throughout all my studies, the theme of Oneness with All That Is was paramount. Was that just a topic that intrigued me or is that the ultimate prize I could have? What did all this inner work look like and how did it change my life? I share within these pages what happened on my path and how people and events showed up to light up my path to my Messiah Within.

## The Significance of Step 1—A Conversation with Yeshua

**Robin:** Yeshua, I love the words of Step 1: *From your deepest point of stillness, find your inner voice that is whispering, "You are One with All."* If we were to break the phrase into its components, each component could stand alone and yet, in order to achieve this knowing, you must view them as a whole phrase. For example, *from your deepest point of stillness* is required so that you can hear *or find your inner voice*. Once you find your inner voice, you need to listen so that you can hear it *whispering, "You are One with All,"* Would you like to elaborate on this exquisite phrase and its role on the path to your Messiah Within?

*Yeshua: The words "You are One with All" are an energetic beacon that is housed in the heart center of each man, woman and child on your planet. The goal of finding your still point is to be able to hear your inner voice (which is the beacon) that is whispering, "You are One with All." Why is it whispering and not shouting it from every core fiber of your being? Because if it were shouting, it would become just another phrase that made its way into your mainstream consciousness without doing the required work to understand its true essence.*

*A good example of this is The Golden Rule. Did you know that there is a Golden Rule for every religious and spiritual group on the planet? "Do unto others as you would have them do unto you" is by far the most common interpretation of this global declaration. Yet, we don't live up to the words themselves. If we did, we would not be having this conversation nor would I have requested you to write this book. If you don't hear the calling that "You are One with All," then what would drive someone to find inner peace, follow The Golden Rule and ultimately contribute to a collective world peace?*

**Robin:** Throughout this process, you have asked me to view your teachings as a fellow Jew. One of the questions that lingers in my mind is whether the Jewish people's recognition of their individual Messiahs Within will create a cultural shift of a desire to be in Oneness with all of Mankind—friends and foes alike. We have discussed that the achievement of a state of Oneness is a critical component of a new global energetic position called the Messiah Consciousness. The Messiah Consciousness may indeed help us to establish and sustain an era of world peace. In the Jewish community, caring for each other and our neighbors is a required Mitzvah (or commandment from HaShem) but it seems to have a significant "internal" emphasis and then "external" after we have taken care of our own community. Can you talk about the Golden Rule and the Torah?

**Yeshua:** *Two of the most common versions of the Golden Rule in the Torah are, "You shall not take vengeance or bear a grudge against your kinsfolk. Love your neighbor as yourself: I am the LORD." Leviticus 19:18. The stranger who resides with you shall be to you as one of your citizens; you shall love him as yourself, for you were strangers in the land of Egypt: I the LORD am your God. Leviticus 19:34 But the great Sage Hillel summed it up beautifully when he* wrote, *"That which is hateful to you, do not do to your fellow. That is the whole Torah; the rest is commentary; go and learn."* Talmud, Shabbat 31a.

*How can we expect an entire race of people to see the light of Oneness after thousands of years of persecution? We tread softly and remind each person that the fastest path to Oneness and world peace is to find it within his or her self first. Once they are filled with light, then let the beacon shine out from within to each person that they encounter (including those with negative intentions towards them).*

*It may sound like an impossible task when we are talking about world peace but as you learned in your process, "A journey of a thousand miles begins with a single step." This famous quote from Lao-tzu, the Chinese Philosopher, emphasizes that the first and single most important step in the journey to your Messiah Within is to hear the calling that "You are One with All That is." Get quiet in whatever manner works for you—meditation, prayer, walking, resting, or gardening—and listen for our words. I promise you that once you truly hear them; your life will never be the same again.*

**Robin:** Thank you, Yeshua. Shalom for now!

**Step One—A Practical Guide: From your deepest point of stillness, find your inner voice that is whispering, "You are One with All"**

1. Identify a location that brings you serenity.
2. Turn off all your electronic communication equipment.
3. Close your eyes and take a few deep breaths to center yourself.
4. Ask your Divine Source to be present with you using prayer or internal conversation.
5. Ask your Spiritual Support Team to help you quiet your mind and open your heart center.
6. As you listen with your heart, hear the words, "You are One with All."
7. Hear these words over and over in your heart center.
8. Honor the energy of the words by sitting in reverence to the Divine and All Being.
9. Express your gratitude to your Divine Source for supporting you as you reach this important milestone on your journey.
10. From this day forth, allow the words "You are One with All" to become a mantra or a phrase that you repeat throughout your day to recognize the divinity in yourself and others.

# *Step Two*

*Identify the spiritual path that is in greatest resonance*
*with your inner knowing*

Jewish Mysticism has been an active religious and spiritual learning model for thousands of years. For the majority of its existence, the study of Kabbalah (a formalized discipline within Jewish Mysticism) has been limited to, and closely held by, the following demographic: Jewish married men over the age of 40 who were Torah students. Prior to the destruction of the Second Temple in 586 C.E., many of the teachings of the Torah were only shared in oral format. Kabbalah literally means "to receive." The oral mystical interpretation of the Torah is found within Kabbalah. Therefore, if you were not involved in Torah study, it was highly unlikely that you would have learned Kabbalah. However, I found an exception to this general understanding in a book that I will share later in this chapter.

In the 1960s, many secular Jewish men and women (like many cross-cultural people in that time) became interested in finding a more spiritual light for their religious studies. Because Kabbalah was not open to all Jews, many began to study the more esoteric eastern philosophies. The Jewish population was small and the rabbis of that time did not want to add yet another reason for Jews to lose active participation in the mainstream Jewish way of life. The rabbis have since decided to open up the teaching of Kabbalah to anyone who expresses an interest.

I grew up in a Jewish home and we had wonderful traditions centered on the Jewish holidays. My husband grew up in a more Conservative Jewish home where attendance at Synagogue and continuing Jewish education was more strongly encouraged. Together, we have been able to find traditions for our own Jewish home that work for both of us. We each observe the Sabbath in our own way and enjoy blending our Jewish heritage with our overall spiritual path.

As a child, I went to Hebrew and Public schools and I had a Bat Mitzvah, but I was not well-educated in Torah studies nor even knew how to read Hebrew well. I decided that I wanted to study Kabbalah anyway. I loved studying Kabbalah and how I could simultaneously learn about my Jewish identity more deeply while moving further along on my study of all things spiritual.

I was in my second year of study when it came time to begin planning my daughter's Bat Mitzvah. Both my husband and now my daughter were well-educated in Hebrew and I was feeling intimidated due to my limited background, so I decided to focus on the celebratory aspects of her Bat Mitzvah. However, my spiritual guidance did not find this path acceptable.

One night, I awoke at 1:00 a.m. to a verbal message from an ethereal female voice. Her words were "In order to reach your next level of spiritual development, you must read the book, *The Rebbe's Daughter.*" I decided to get up and write myself a note. Thank goodness I did, because the next day I found the note on my briefcase. I might not have remembered it in the morning, and I was grateful that I had recognized the importance of this message even in my most sleepy state. I carried the note to my corporate office like the treasure that it was.

I turned on my computer and went online to a book-seller. I typed in the words, "The Rebbe's Daughter" and behold a book appeared. I was completely shocked and ordered it immediately. As I researched the author, I discovered that he had been walking by a bookstore in Israel when he saw a diary on a shelf. He went in and found it to be the diary of one of the daughters of a noted Chassidic Master from pre-World War I in Central Europe. In the book, Malkah Shapiro (the Rebbe's Daughter) awakens to spirituality and religious consciousness in a unique place and time. The memoir is translated and presented by Rabbi Nehamia Polen. But, I kept thinking, "What does this have to do with me?"

I read this book word-by-word. I even read every footnote, trying to find that one magic piece of information that would change my life forever. I learned about what it meant to be a young Chassidic girl preparing for her Bat Mitzvah in the early 1900s. I learned how important the study of the Torah was to Chassidic women; how, after they finished their chores, they sat in their own study groups and discovered the amazing teachings of the Torah. This was so new to me. I thought this type of worshipful study was available only to men in the Chassidic community. It gave me an entirely new viewpoint and respect for Chassidic women. They are not forbidden from study or daily prayer; but they are excused from daily prayer because their role as mother to the children is the highest priority.

After reading the book, I discovered a greater passion for Judaism and I learned about the true significance of the Bat Mitzvah ceremony. I became interested in not only learning fundamental Hebrew prayers, but also learning to read from the Torah so that I could join my daughter on the Bimah (the sacred podium which stands before the ark that houses the Torah scrolls) and, in essence, truly have my own Bat Mitzvah. This act of reading from the Torah enabled me to fully embrace my identity as a Jew. Now that I was becoming comfortable with my spiritual identity as a Jew, I could truly dive into my extensive path of spiritual study.

## The Significance of Step 2—A Conversation with Yeshua

**Robin:** Yeshua, I would say that this was truly the beginning of my journey to finding my Messiah Within. When I heard the female voice in the middle of the night—well, quite frankly, I knew I was not alone anymore! Why did the journey begin here?

**Yeshua:** Yes, Robin, you are correct—this is where the journey began for you because it was important for you to re-kindle your

Jewish Spiritual identity for three main reasons. The first was for you to have a strong foundation for writing this book. The second was to establish a spiritual direction or compass for finding your Messiah Within. The third was to give you an anchor for your vessel during the tremendous spiritual storm that would be a requirement for your personal spiritual journey.

**Robin:** I loved this book *The Rebbe's Daughter*. I read every word, every footnote—I could not get enough. I even read the last chapter twice so that the book would not end. Beyond that I was spiritually guided to read it, why did I feel so connected to Malkah Shapiro and her experience as a young Chassidic woman? It would be so easy for me to think that this was a past life for me but, intuitively, that did not quite feel right. Can you explain the connection between Malkah and me?

*Yeshua: It was really not about your connection with Malkah—she was just the character in the story. The true connection was to the Chassidic people and their devotion to Torah. We wanted you to see just how critical the Torah was and how sacred was the information contained in it. It was like showing you the existence of a treasure map. We wanted you to become proud of being a Jew. At this time, we also began to re-awaken your husband's Ori's deep love for Judaism so that he could become a teacher for you on this part of your path. We are deeply pleased with his growth in this area and his acceptance of his role, albeit unofficial, as a rabbi or teacher of Judaism. Remember that in my lifetime, a rabbi was a revered teacher, not a formal clergy person (yet!). Ori has this rabbinic energy and he is an important resource for you.*

**Robin:** In the answer to my first question above, you said that I needed to establish my Jewish spiritual identity as a compass for finding my Messiah Within. Is this a requirement for all of Mankind to find their spiritual identity in order to find their Messiah Within?

*Yeshua:* *The answer to that is both yes and no. Yes, it is vitally important for people to recognize their spiritual path in order to walk on it towards their Messiah Within. But what is not required is that they follow a religious or commonly accepted spiritual path. They can find the path to their Messiah Within by staying committed to whatever brings them their greatest joy and wherever they can practice unconditional love. Religious and spiritual teachers are here to light up the path to the Messiah Within. But if you know how to stay on the path and do not require a more formal doctrine, then so be it.*

**Robin:** Thank you, Yeshua. Shalom for now!

**Step Two—A Practical Guide: Identify the spiritual path that is in greatest resonance with your inner knowing**

1. Reflect on your life to discover what gives you the greatest level of joy.
2. Is this activity (identified in the step above) one that can enable you to grow to greater spiritual connection or bring you closer to your own inner divinity?
3. If yes, wonderful! If no, let's dive a little deeper. Can you recall a particular theme in spiritual books or personal development classes that you took or an activity (such as hiking in nature) that truly resonated with you?
4. Once you have identified that which truly resonated with you, determine if you are open to pursuing this activity in greater detail and with more commitment.
5. Are you willing to eliminate all the excuses for not getting on your path? Please nod your head "yes" if you are ready.
6. Great! Determine how best to make a deeper commitment and move onto your path with joy and passion.
7. How will you know you are on the path? Simple: your life will become easier because you are going with the flow of the universal energies. No more paddling upstream!
8. Revel in the unconditional love from your Spiritual Support Team as they begin to guide you on your path.
9. Express your gratitude to the Divine for leading you to and down the path.
10. Share the unconditional love that is being shared with you with others. Pay it forward!

# Step Three

*Become your Authentic Self*

For twenty-five years, I worked in Corporate America. I enjoyed a career filled with interesting jobs and met interesting people. I was referred to unofficially, of course, as "The Mayor" of my company for engaging and treating all employees with friendly respect and dignity, no matter what their level. Around my twenty-second year in Corporate America, I decided to jump off the "corporate ladder" and take a temporary staff position in the Corporate Education department doing special projects for the senior leadership team. It was in this position that I learned about the concept of "Spirit at Work" and how successful companies were infusing their companies with spirit to achieve better financial results. What an interesting idea . . . treat your employees with respect and integrity and they work more creatively and efficiently, and the end result is a more enhanced bottom line!

It was through my interactions with fellow colleagues who were interested in applying the concept of Spirit at Work that I decided to become my Authentic Self at work. What did this mean, Authentic Self? At the time, I had two personalities, one was my corporate personality and the other was my spiritual warrior one. As the spiritual warrior, I would attend spiritual and wellness retreats on the weekend and read all kinds of books on a variety of "out there" topics. However, I was reluctant to let my two personalities merge at work. At the time, Spirituality, like Sex, was an "S word" that you could not talk about in Corporate America. Therefore, I wondered how I would speak about it and how it might affect my career.

As I became my Authentic Self, I began to develop a knowing that I was destined to do some type of work that was much bigger than my corporate career and would allow me to be of great service to many more people. It was fun and entertaining, becoming my Authentic Self at work. If someone asked me what I did on the weekend, instead of my standard line, "hung out with my family, did the laundry, etc." I began to tell them what I actually did. "I went to a Past Life Regression workshop." After they picked their jaws up off their chests, inevitably they would say, "Really? Let me tell you what I'm into." This became *de facto* market research for my new entrepreneurial endeavor. What I discovered was that everyday people are into spiritual teachings and most felt that they had to hide their attraction to this type of learning.

During my final three years in Corporate America, every six months my work Director would say, "Time to find a full time job. But WAIT, how about this new project?" I would take on each suggested project because it allowed me great opportunities to work with the senior executive level, seeing the very big picture. And a secondary benefit was that it allowed me important insights about how to build a business plan for my own company-to-be. What I also knew for sure was that there was no full-time job coming in my corporate career—my spiritual guidance had grander plans for me.

I began to think about and seriously plan my own company. Through a healing process called Transformational Breathwork, I was able to reach very deep states of meditation and relaxation, which allowed me to access my inner wisdom. Now, I had lots of work to do—and I was torn by my deep attachment to my corporate persona and the gratitude I felt for my personal development under the auspices of my employer. Furthermore, I had no idea how to become an entrepreneur or how to function without the support systems I had become used to having provided in my corporate job.

I had one other great obstacle at this time and that was convincing my husband that it was okay to leave my very secure job, to forfeit one-half of our family income, all to *heal the world*. Ori and I travelled to Omega Institute for a Qi Qong weekend retreat. At this weekend, Ori saw that all the attendees were indeed everyday people and that they were going out of their way to enhance their spiritual growth and their wellness. He saw and understood my vision to provide this type of information locally in Connecticut. He was "in" and became my partner in our new company.

In the early stages of our company, we ran weekly events showcasing local spiritual and wellness professionals in our area and supported Spiritual Cinema film makers in distributing their films worldwide. It was challenging and fun and the freedom that I felt not being confined to a corporate office was exhilarating. A dear friend once told me, "there is life outside of Corporate America" and he was so right.

On my bookshelf, I have a small drawing that I made during that transition year of a very happy girl divided into the various aspects of her Divine self. She has Divine Light pouring out of the top of the head with Divine Knowledge filling the corners of her mind, Divine Love expanding into—and out of—her heart, and she is sharing Divine Information with the community at large. I made this picture to share with my mother so that she would not think that I had completely lost my mind in leaving my successful corporate career. I smile at the picture even today because it is still so relevant in my private client work and the work of all of the enlightened professionals who work with us. At that time it was just a sketch, an intellectual concept; today it is the core concept of my life's work—and our business is named "Enlightened Professionals."

## The Significance of Step 3—A Conversation with Yeshua

**Robin:** When I first looked at this chapter, I thought there was nothing I could ask you about—nothing spiritual happening here in my life—but then I had a good laugh. I recognized a very important step, which was becoming one's Authentic Self. What does "becoming one's Authentic Self" mean?

Robin H. Clare

*Yeshua: To become one's Authentic Self means to stand in your personal power and take pride in your ideals, desires and actions on your path. We come into this world with expectations that are placed upon us by our parents, our teachers, our religious leaders, our bosses, our siblings, our children, our friends. These expectations influence the choices that we make as young adults, as we begin to establish a plan for our future. In the materialistic world in which we live, most young adults are encouraged to find a career that is lucrative but not necessarily joyful. As you can recall in your life, Robin, your father said that you can be a doctor, a lawyer or an accountant. You chose the accountant because it was the least amount of school. And you truly disliked it but you did it anyway. Of course, along the way you began to move into more passionate areas of pursuit, into roles within Human Resources and Event Production. But as you have seen in your company, all of the skills that you learned were critical to your success.*

**Robin:** As the parent of a young adult and a teenager, I truly want to influence my children to take career paths that will bring them the most joy because I know that the more joyful they are, the more they have a chance of attracting abundance into their lives. However, the cost of college is so high that you want them to be able to quickly make a decent living so they can assist with paying back their college loans. Do you see the conundrum facing parents today?

*Yeshua: Well, first of all, we have stepped forward from requiring our children to be doctors, lawyers and accountants, and may I say that expectation was very prevalent in Jewish families. This is because education is of very high importance within the Jewish community and correlates directly back to the Jews and the Torah. For centuries, the most revered member of any Jewish community was the Torah scholar. For those who could not be a Torah scholar it was, and is still, revered to be the best scholar of whatever it was you were learning. Whether it was for you to become a doctor or a shoemaker, you learned your trade well and you performed to you highest potential. That is why I have such great hopes for the Jewish community today, to embrace the teachings of Oneness and to see how much they can influence the world as they have done with their advancements in the sciences and the humanities and other innovations on the Earth plane.*

*Now, back to your question, I think that you truly answered it for yourself. Life is not about who has the biggest and the best toys. Your husband has a wonderful saying when your children would complain that their friends had bigger and better homes, he would say, "We don't know how much money someone has or makes, we can only see what they spend it on." We liked this saying because it was teaching your children to value what is important to them. What is more important is that they live a life of balance. There should be no distinction between their work and their personal life—it is just their life, their authentic life. So, whether at home or at work, they need to approach it from an attitude of joy that allows them to feel they are being of service and making a difference in the lives of those they interact with on a daily basis.*

*Finding this important balance requires that they be in a perpetual state of joy. A joyful persona is very attractive in both one's personal and professional relationships. Truly, how can more come to you if you are in a state of fear that you don't have enough? That is counter-intuitive to the Law of Attraction. We attract what we are thinking, feeling and acting upon. If you worry about paying the bills, the Universe will send you less money, because all you can think about is "not enough" and the Universe responds to "not enough" by bringing you "not enough." Abraham-Hicks has a great quote, "Worrying is like praying for what you don't want."*

*So, for the college-bound children on the Earth today, we encourage you to study what you love to learn. This will set the stage for a career doing what you love, which will in turn provide you with an abundant living that will in turn pay your college loans!*

Robin H. Clare

**Robin:** In a deep meditation today, you reminded me that becoming my Authentic Self is required at each step of my development on my spiritual path. You advised me that I needed to fully step into and live my current work. While I always approach every next phase of my development with curiosity and commitment, I always have a difficult time truly accepting these next levels of gifts. Can you help me to understand why?

*Yeshua: We promise that we are not laughing at you, Robin, but this question is rather amusing. For ten years, you have made every leap we have asked of you gladly, but—aha! I have it—you have made every leap only if you saw a safety net beneath you. For you this has come in the form of taking on work assignments that have distracted you and have prevented you from focusing on your true purpose and have continued to foster relationships that don't enable you to fly fully. We would ask you to go back and remember all the times you just completely took a true leap of FAITH. What happened? That's right, the outcome was greater than you could have possibly imagined! It is when you have to think it through and think that you have to plan things completely that you don't allow the work to flow from your heart center or your connection to the Divine. We ask all of you to "think from your heart" not your head—we promise you a greater outcome!*

*At each of your development phases of your life (not just your spiritual journey), and in response to your desire to be successful in any given pursuit, we always provide you with the gifts to do exceptionally well. What has typically happened, though, is that you are not always in a state of "allowing" or may at that moment be incapable of receiving our gifts. Why is that? Very simply, you do not feel worthy of them. And why not? Because somewhere in your ego, a voice is telling you, "This cannot be so, and, how could I be worthy of this?" Please listen carefully: you are all amazing human beings and are capable of greatness in your lives. From simply loving your family and friends in an unconditional manner to a*

38

*career that changes the course of history, your contribution is vitally important to the fabric of our Universe. Would we bestow these gifts unto you if we did not have complete confidence in you to use them appropriately?*

**Robin:** Thank you, Yeshua. Shalom for now!

## Step 3—A Practical Guide: Become your Authentic Self

1. Define for yourself what being your Authentic Self would look like for you.
2. Compare and contrast the characteristics of your Authentic Self to the persona that you are living today.
3. Review the situations in your life where it would be easiest to start moving into your Authentic Self.
4. If you find that there are none, begin to seek out like-minded friends through like-minded organizations.
5. If you find that you can only be your Authentic Self with a certain person or in one group, look for ways to spend more time with that individual or group.
6. As you begin to feel more comfortable with your Authentic Self, you will want to become this person in a greater percentage of your life.
7. Determine ways in your life that you can expand the time that you get to be your Authentic Self.
8. Be brave and know that you will attract to you like-minded people when you stand in the power of who you truly are.
9. Be open to know that some current friends and family may struggle with the new "you" for a while or forever; that is their choice and they will adapt to the new "you" if they choose to.
10. As often as you can, represent yourself from the true power of your Authentic Self—know and speak your truth from your highest and best good. The more you do it, the easier it gets!

# Step Four

*Allow the Universe to provide you with what you need*
*for your growth, alignment and well-being*

In 2007, I was traveling with my family to Florida for a family reunion and I was reading a spiritually oriented magazine. There was a tiny article entitled *Can 64,000 People Become Enlightened by the Year 2012?* It was an article about the Oneness University and Sri AmmaBhagavhan, its founders. It was a tiny article but it stirred me. The article talked about how Sri AmmaBhagavhan are Avatars of Awakening Consciousness on the planet and that they had a university in India, where you could learn to be a Oneness Blessing Giver. The Oneness Blessing (or "Deeksha" as it is referred to in India) is a transfer of Divine grace that enables folks to quiet the mind, thus allowing them to live from their heart center or in an awakened state. I looked at my husband, Ori, across the aisle and I said, "Maybe I'm supposed to go to India—ha ha."

The next week, I was having a private channeling session and I asked the channel, "Is Deeksha real?" She smiled and with that a surge of energy started at the base of my feet and traveled all the way up to the top of my head. It hurt, but we laughed because I knew that the Deeksha was real, indeed! My guidance in the session was that I was being called to India to begin my path to awakening. I had no idea what this meant and I had no idea how I was going to convince my husband that I had to go. My spiritual guidance shared that I had to stand in my own personal power and just inform Ori that I was going. I was not to engage in a debate or look for permission; I was to execute my Divine will. It was not up for negotiation—I had to go. They, in turn would work with Ori to reach a place of understanding of my need to go on this trip and they would help me find the money.

Please know that this is not the way our relationship worked at the time. Everything was a compromise, everything was discussed at length and decisions were made that were in the highest and best good of our entire family. We have now learned that this is not how spiritual path decisions are made—we now provide each other with the space, flexibility and understanding to determine how best to use our resources (personal energy, time and funding) for our spiritual growth.

We were both sitting at our desks in our home office and I said, "I'm going to India—I'm being called to go." Ori turned and looked at me and said, "That's it—no discussion, no seeking consensus?" I said, "I have no choice, I have to go." He asked, "How will you pay for this?" and I answered, "The money will arrive." Ok, yes, he did think I had lost my sense of reality, but here is what happened next . . .

The next day, my first husband called me and asked if I could meet him for breakfast. I said, "Of course" and I met him. My first husband is a successful financial planner and he wanted to tell me that there was a new rule that enabled me to withdraw money from one of my investment vehicles without penalty. I said, "Really, how much?" and he said, "$10,000." You guessed it—the exact cost of the trip to India!

It was truly at this time that I started to recognize that when you are in the flow of your own Divine path, miracles do happen—even what might be considered a minor one like finding the money to go to India—just like that!

I now could go to India but was I willing to stretch beyond the confines of our marriage to move along my path in such a significant way? I had made my decision, but it was, nonetheless, difficult. The "Ori of then" just did not understand this need in me to go. Now, I can look back at that stressful time and smile because the "Ori of today," a man deeply committed to his own spiritual path, would understand and bless me on my path. At that time, not so much. But we survived it (barely).

I consulted with a friend who had been to the Oneness University twice so she would act as my guide on how to prepare and thrive in India. India is an amazing country, but it is totally unique and requires you to prepare mentally, physically, emotionally and spiritually. In that land of great spirituality, there is also great poverty and you need to prepare for many situations like finding antibiotics, ways to cleanse your water and secure your important documents.

At this time, I was introduced to a man who would come to play an important role in my life. He would travel with me to India for the three weeks at the Oneness University. The experience of being in India together at the Oneness University created a bond that grew deeper as the years progressed. I purchased my ticket, got my shots, packed for a month's stay, and I was ready to go! Ori dropped me off at the airport for my twenty-two hour flight. I was flying from Hartford to Amsterdam, Amsterdam to Frankfurt, Germany and Germany to Chennai, India. I was excited and I was scared.

## The Significance of Step 4—A Conversation with Yeshua

**Robin:** This time in my life was huge in regards to standing on the ledge and jumping and not knowing if there was a net that was going to catch me. Why did you send this "nice Jewish girl" to India, of all places?

**Yeshua:** *This was not a sending to India, this was a returning home to India. For you see, Robin, while you have spent lifetimes as a Jew, you have also spent lifetimes as a Hindu. In fact, you were a very revered spiritual teacher who basically lost his mind in the passion of his beliefs. Do you recall the Indian man that you met in a hypnosis session? That was you from lifetimes ago, and it was important for you to release him from your current energy field. He was highly regarded for his knowledge of Oneness and yet, his mind became* *confused. When you saw him he was disoriented, but you knew that he was deeply loved by his followers who cared for him. You asked us in the session to bring him into the light and to have him be at peace. The process was critical for you and it began in India. In India, you would be introduced to the culture and the concepts that were critical to that lifetime and critical to your personal learning and teachings in this lifetime. We applaud you loudly for going. That, my friend, was indeed a huge leap for you.*

**Robin:** Yes, I thought you would have sent me to Israel before sending me to India.

**Yeshua:** *Well, "the nice Jewish girl" did go to India and we made this very apparent to you in your travel experience and in two scenarios in India. Let's first discuss your air travel. We sent you through Germany so that you could feel the energy of the Holocaust in your emotional body. As you boarded the plane in Germany, you began to feel ill and you were violently ill for the entire nine hours to Chennai. You had to release the fear of the Holocaust that was so prevalent in your emotional structure and this had to be done quickly. We are sorry that it was so hard, but you needed to be ready to accept all that India was going to throw at you, including meeting someone whom you greatly feared in your Holocaust lifetime.*

*Do you remember meeting her? She came into your dorm room and you became scared once more and she knew it. She took the last bed and that was the one next to yours. You both were required to address your Holocaust experience together, to learn tolerance for each other, for, you see, you were both Jews in the Holocaust. Do you recall that you did not believe her that she was a Jew in the Holocaust because of how uneasy she made you feel? That was because she was, for lack of a better term, a snitch. She would turn in her fellow Jews in order to protect herself. As you later learned, you did your best to deny that you were Jewish during the Holocaust. So, here we placed together the snitch and the denier—quite a combination, the two of you were. In either case, you both garnered complete and utter fear and shame from that lifetime. In India, with the help of a woman from Israel, you would all heal together as you recognized your lifetime together and how HaShem had brought you all together in a very special place, The Oneness University.*

**Robin:** Then why was I so sick on the way back to Germany? The moment I stepped into the airport at Chennai, I was ill. Not a pretty sight as I was crawling through Indian Customs!

*Yeshua: Sorry to say that you were sick on the way back for a whole different reason. You became so filled with energy that we needed to "release the valve" a lot before you could return to your life with Ori and your children. This will become more apparent in the next two chapters. We ask your patience to wait for more clarity.*

**Robin:** I was clearly going as a Jew to India and I felt more connected to my Judaism in India than I had ever felt at home. I must have said the Shema (our twice daily prayer), at least ten times a day. Was I just trying to maintain my identity or was there some deeper explanation?

*Yeshua: Thank you for asking this because this is important for your readers. On the path to becoming your Messiah Within, you must identify your spiritual path—yours is in Judaism. However, that does not mean that you cannot be open to the teachings of other great paths with teachings that resonate with you. In order to reach a state of Oneness on the planet, we must all be open to have complete acceptance of another's path. The Shema gave you peace in your heart and connected you to your home and your people when you felt alone or were engaged in deep healing that was such an intricate part of your India experience. So on one hand, you were trying to maintain your identity and it was easy at The Oneness University.*

*For after all, Sri AmmaBhagavhan understand completely that the end goal is to get to a state of Oneness. They presented you with their Hindu perspective but they truly honor all paths and made it comfortable for you to embrace yours while embracing their teachings. We knew that this was the perfect place for you to begin—thank you for following the breadcrumbs placed out for you!*

**Robin:** Two other important lessons that I learned during this time were to stand in my personal power with Ori and to also be in a state of allowing in order to receive the funding to go. Would you care to comment on either of these?

**Yeshua:** *Yes, let's clarify the situation with Ori. We were not asking you to stand in your personal power with Ori; we were asking you to stand in your personal power period. Ori was just a minor obstacle to get around. You were the bigger obstacle. It was easier to make it about Ori than to have you deal with your own issues of personal power at that time. Quite frankly, you were not ready to stand in your own personal power and walk bravely on your path. You walked on your path, but not so bravely, but you walked and we honor you for that.*

*Ah, your first husband, what a kind soul. He was very surprised when we tapped him on the shoulder to call you and give you the information about the money you required to make this life changing trip. Here is how manifesting the funds works: an idea is conceived by you of something that you desire, you set your intention to receive it, the Universe sets in motion opportunities to achieve your desire, you decide to ALLOW the desire to be fulfilled and it is fulfilled. But here is the trick: the Universe will provide for both what you most desire and what you least desire. The Universe will "just provide" whatever you place your attention on, so be careful what you ask for! If you like, you may include as the practical guide for Step 4 the Universal Road Map that we shared with you to help you understand the Law of Attraction and the Art of Allowing.*

**Robin:** Thank you, Yeshua. Shalom for now!

## Step 4—A Practical Guide: The Universal Road Map

1. The first step on your journey is to become **calm** and **centered** so that you can hear your *inner voice.*

2. Once you clearly hear your inner voice/wisdom, you begin to set an **intention** for *your highest and best outcomes.*

3. From your point of clear intention, you can begin to **develop** a strategy or plan to reach your highest potential.

4. A most important step is to **align** your *thoughts with words and actions* that support your strategy for success.

5. The alignment of thoughts, words and actions creates a **vibration**, a unique energetic request that *you can now fulfill.*

6. Individuals and opportunities having a **vibrational match** to yours will *come into your life.*

7. The key to your *knowing* how a vibrational match may be beneficial to you is to fully understand the **resonance** between you.

8. By **allowing** yourself to receive the opportunities presented to you, you will achieve your plan and the abundance you desire.

# *Step Five*

*Heal your relationships with your immediate family*

I remember watching Ori's face as I was heading towards the security gates at Bradley Airport. He looked like he thought he would never see me again. I was not sure that he would either. Traveling internationally was scary enough after 9/11, but I had no idea what was going to happen to me. Would I even come back as the same person? Would Ori recognize me? Would I recognize myself?

After 22 hours and three different planes, I landed in Chennai, India. I found my luggage and met a woman who would become my friend at the Oneness University. We met our travel guide and we had the most wonderful chai tea outside of the airport. Our guide placed us in a taxi (around 2:00 a.m.) and off we went on the 2-hour ride to the Oneness University. What we did not know is that there are very few traffic rules in India; many cars and trucks leave their lights off when driving at night and cars travelling in opposite directions often drive on the same side of the road. The only way order is maintained is by everyone honking their horns for the whole trip. There we were, in the back seat of this taxi, freaking out every time a car or truck came barreling down our lane at us with their lights off. The taxi driver kept laughing at us, saying, "Everything is fine, Ma'am!"

We finally arrived and I had not slept in more than 24 hours. I made my way to my cot and slept for about five hours. My new friend and I awoke at the same time and we had the whole day to explore, rest and meet the other attendees. What we discovered is that there were people attending the Oneness University from all over the world. We were in the English-speaking group and there were two other groups, one from Italy and one from Japan. It was the most exciting experience of my life. I could not believe I was in India, meeting people from across the globe. We were here for three weeks and it would become the longest and the shortest three weeks of my life.

On the first day of our workshops, the head Dasa (teacher/monk) came to speak to us first. More than two hundred English-speaking attendees sat either on the floor or in chairs anxiously awaiting his first words. He began by saying, "We are so glad you are here. Over the next three weeks, we will provide you with the tools to become HAPPY." A big groan went through the crowd. I guess many folks were looking for enlightenment, the meaning of life or some other abstract concept. I laughed out loud, thinking of the credit card commercial, "Happiness, priceless." I thought, "Heck, yeah, I'll take happiness!" If I could leave after three weeks and be happy all the time, what more could I ask for? I was ready to do some serious work to achieve a state of happiness. I had no idea how hard it was going to be. Ori thought I was just going on vacation, but this was no visit to the Taj Mahal!

We spent three weeks learning the teachings of Sri AmmaBhagavhan, meditating with Oneness Beings (individuals in high states of consciousness), doing Inner Child work (healing the wounds of our childhood), resting and spending a considerable amount of time in silence. We ate, we rested, we walked, but were not supposed to talk. My new girlfriend and I wrote notes back and forth. But my friend from home, a man whom you will read more about later—that was a different story. We would sneak up on the roof to chit-chat and make each other laugh. I truly tried to be in silence, but I just was not good at it.

I worked on my childhood issues and relationship issues with my parents and my spouse. I reviewed my parenting skills—I looked at it all under an intense spiritual microscope powered by Sri AmmaBhagavhan. In deep meditation and through the power of the Deeksha energy provided, I was able to interact with my parents as if I was still a child, but seeing them through the eyes of the "adult

Robin." What an experience to see your childhood through your parents' perspective. It makes you realize they could never be perfect and they were only human, just like you. It allows you to forgive them on a very deep level. It was powerful and exhausting, but I would never trade that experience for anything. At the heart of Sri AmmaBhagavhan's teachings is that we must heal our relationships with our parents before we can reach our greatest spiritual and life potential. By doing the self-examination there, I set the stage for the next four years of healings and experiences that would bring me to my Messiah Within.

Upon my return to the States, Ori and the kids met me at Bradley Airport. Hailey, my dog, greeted me at the door like I had just been away for three weeks—an abundance of kisses and hugs! We were all excited and I shared my gifts with them. All was peaceful for the night. And then, the next morning, the phone rang.

## The Significance of Step 5—A Conversation with Yeshua

**Robin:** How can we best explain my extraordinary experience at the Oneness University? I'm laughing because trying to explain this is like trying to explain to new parents what it will be like when their first infant child arrives!

*Yeshua: Yes, that's a great analogy and to complicate the explanation even more is that your experience was unique to you. No one else had that same experience or ever will. Before I answer your question, I would like to focus on this concept of how each person's experience on the spiritual path is unique to him or her. Therefore, by its very design, being unique would hold no space for judgment or placing a value of right or wrong. When people are dedicated to the path of becoming their Messiah Within, they need to be open to considering any direction they are shown by their Spiritual Support Team. We used the word "consider" versus "accept" because, as always, you have free will to change the course. Just be careful with that and ensure you are changing the course from a place of rational thought rather than fear. We promise you that we will never give you growth opportunities that you can't handle. Our goal is to provide you with the greatest gift available to humanity and that is to bring Heaven to Earth. And that requires considerable trust and faith on your path.*

*Now back to your question, The Oneness University, like many spiritual ashrams, is a place of deep reflection. Going to an ashram is not for the faint of heart. The Oneness University was established by Sri AmmaBhagavhan as a place for individuals to attend, to push them along their path to Oneness. Individuals who attended the Oneness University came with different intentions about how they would influence others on their path to Oneness. For some, it was as simple as bringing these teachings into their home and workplace, for others it was required reflection on their path to teaching about Oneness. Either way, the experience was unique for each person.*

*For you, Robin, the experience brought you great growth in many ways. Beyond standing in your own power and dealing with a Holocaust past-life trauma as we described in the previous chapter, the true teachings took place, as you so eloquently said, "under an intense spiritual microscope powered by Sri AmmaBhagavhan." For serious spiritual seekers, you MUST heal your relationships with your parents and those whom you love the most dearly on this planet. The traumas created in this lifetime (and past lifetimes) will prevent you from seeing clearly these loved ones in a state of Oneness. If you cannot see the people you love (or those you may hate, in some cases) in Oneness, how can you expect to see the world in Oneness? The process of Oneness and world peace begins within **you**.*

*When you can clearly see these people with warts and all, then you can accept them without judgment. When you stop taking their giving or denying of love as a barometer of your own self-worth, then you can accept yourself without judgment. This is not easy, but it is required on the path to becoming your Messiah Within. How each of you will do this work is up to you, there is no right or wrong way, but we highly recommend that you connect with a Spiritual Support*

*Team on the Earth plane and beyond. Once you intuitively know whom to trust to help you with this intense work on your path, honor and trust that the relationship was established for your highest and best good. Know that you will be surrounded by Divine energies that are so proud of you and will guide you during this exhilarating and exhausting time.*

**Robin:** Most people are afraid of dealing with the pain of childhood or adult traumas and when you combine that with the Ego that wants to make sure we stay protected from pain, how does one get beyond these two obstacles to look at his or her traumatic experiences?

*Yeshua: If you don't mind, we are going to throw this question back to you, Robin. What made you have the courage to do your Inner Child work and heal your relationships with your loved ones?*

**Robin:** This is a very tough question. No wonder you threw it back to me! Is it because we are tired of being in pain or is it because we intuitively know that there is a better existence than pain and we are willing to look at all of our "issues" in order to have a better existence? For me, I noticed that while in the midst of the Inner Child and relationship work, there was great pain in remembering and feeling those forgotten feelings. But the relief I felt and the joy I felt after the true meaning of the issue was revealed to me was far greater than the pain itself. It was as if I finally learned the important lesson from that time.

Here is the most important teaching: if I only understood the lesson with my mind and not my heart, then I was not done with the lesson; it would come back again. So, now I am really careful to understand the lesson with my full heart and not just my mind. This important nuance made and continues to make a tremendous difference in my life. Because even after I thought I was done preparing for this book, more lessons were revealed to me and I was able to address them quickly and with accuracy of resolution. I will share those lessons later on in the book, I promise.

As Sri AmmaBhagavhan taught so well, once we quiet the mind and listen with our hearts, situations and problems will still arise, but we become like an observer of the situation and that allows the situation to diffuse more quickly because the knowing of the true meaning comes much quicker. I can't thank you enough for sending me to the Oneness University and to the teachings of Sri AmmaBhagavhan. They have affected my life every day since I was privileged to attend.

*Yeshua: You're welcome, Robin. Shalom for now!*

## Step 5—A Practical Guide: Heal your relationships with your immediate family

1. Give yourself kudos for being open to taking this next step.
2. Seek out a professional individual or organization to guide you through the process.
3. Connect to your Spiritual Support Team to guide you and be with you throughout this process.
4. Ask for guidance on the best order to do this work. For example, start with your parents, then work on your siblings, your partner and your children.
5. Allow yourself the freedom to express how you feel to this person even if he or she is only in an energetic state. Cry, laugh, and yell. It doesn't matter—just express yourself clearly and honestly.
6. Allow yourself to hear why your relationship was the way it was from **their** perspective.
7. Another critical step in the process is to **accept** their perspective **without** judgment. We are not asking you to condone their behavior, just accept it was what they thought at the time was the right thing to do.
8. When you can do the step above, you can accept the person with **unconditional love.**
9. And when you can love unconditionally, you are so very much on your way to becoming your Messiah Within.

# *Step Six*

*Live your life fully without the fear of death*

My trip to India would come to serve many purposes and would be a springboard to many deeply profound experiences in my life. The first one took place within twenty-four hours of being home. The very next morning, my daughter Gaby received a message that two of her friends had been killed in a horrible car accident that also killed two other teens and an adult in the other car.

The experience was surreal. I was still totally blissed out from being in India—yet here I was providing comfort to Gaby and her friends during this time of great distress. Because of my heightened state of consciousness at the time, I was taken to the accident scene and shown that Gaby's friend's mother (who had passed five years before) was there to help all of the teens cross over. I was so confident of this knowing that I shared it with Gaby and her friends.

This heightened state allowed me to truly know that there is no death, there is only the releasing of the physical body. While we are always part of "All that Is," the entire universal flow, our earthly existence makes it difficult for us to remember that. The dense energies of the Earth and the physical requirements of existing on this plane make it difficult to live in the "subtle energies"; not impossible, just harder. When we pass over, we release our physical bodies and merge completely in All Being. Because of just returning from three weeks of meditation and inner transformation, I was consciously part of All Being. Therefore, it was as if I was watching or observing this horrific experience from a state of grace. This grace allowed me to serve as a great source of comfort to Gaby and her friends.

A few years later, Gaby and I were at a Gallery Reading with a talented Medium. One of Gaby's deceased friends from the auto accident and her deceased mother came from the spiritual realm to speak to us. She told Gaby that she had a choice to come back but she chose to stay with her mother who had passed before her. She missed her mom terribly on the Earth plane but now she could be with her in All Being and this was the choice she made. She wanted Gaby to share that with their mutual friends so they all would understand her position. Her mother also thanked me for my support to her daughter's friends during the accident. It was a beautiful confirmation that what I was experiencing at the time was real and how important it is to learn to be a witness and serve as a conduit for the Divine to do their work.

After returning from India, I would also have two more experiences that involved teens and auto accidents. In a dream state, I was taken into the vehicles to assist the teens in crossing over. I experienced the crash with them and had to show them to the light. The experiences in the dream state were scary and in one case the car was consumed in fire. But throughout it all there was a Divine light and grace that brought peace into the car. Why all three accidents? Why was I chosen to provide support to these beautiful souls moving into All Being? I believe that I was chosen because I know that we do not die and I needed to bring that knowing and confidence to each situation, both for the teens crossing over and also for the individuals in mourning on the Earth plane.

As I write this, Japan has just experienced the great earthquake and tsunami of 2011. My knowing is that this is one of many weather-related activities that will create great death and despair on the Earth plane during this time of great shift for Humanity and for the Earth. For those who can grasp the concept of "no death" and passing into All Being, the emotional impact will be far less sad and one of acceptance.

Quite recently, a dear friend of mine passed from illness. When I found out two years ago that she was ill, I cried for hours; I was devastated. At that time, I was in a great state of emotional stress in my personal relationships and in a process of my own internal growth. I was vulnerable to tremendous sadness and I allowed myself to experience it deeply.

When she passed, my son, Garrett, was surprised to see that I was not crying. I typically cry at the least emotional provocation. He asked me why I wasn't crying. While I had an overall sadness and I knew that I would miss my dear friend, I could not help but smile thinking about my friend's crossing over. She was one of the most grace-filled people I had ever known. I knew that she would arrive in "Heaven" in great awe and be welcomed into All Being with unconditional love. I knew that she would know that, too; therefore, her passing would be easy for her. On the day after she passed, I heard her voice say, "Robin, I'm sorry we could not say goodbye, I had to prepare my daughters for my passing." I was feeling sad about not seeing her before she passed, but then I had my confirmation that all was well.

The meaning of life is "to live." How very simple, yet so hard. If we live with the fear of death or with the fear of not accomplishing or with regret, we can only anticipate death with great trepidation. If we know there is no death, that we are only shedding our human body and we have always been in complete Oneness with All Being, then we can approach life with joy and great excitement for the transition to All Being. That is what I know my friend did. I dreamed about her the other day and she was playing and joyful and not riddled with illness. It was great to see her so happy. I wish this peaceful knowing for all of us.

## The Significance of Step 6—A Conversation with Yeshua

**Robin:** I'm not quite sure where to begin. While at times this period on the journey felt so strange and out of the ordinary, in retrospect, it was perhaps what you might call the "new normal." I was able to take this extraordinary connection that I felt to All Being and use it to assist all of these beautiful teens understand what was happening to them. Can you comment on this?

*Yeshua: As I have shared before, death is extremely feared by most of you. This is because the concept of **just** shedding the physical body and returning to All Being is a difficult concept to get our hands around. We emphasized the word **just** above because we want to be clear that we are always part of All **Being** and death is the return to your natural state. Your natural state is the time that you are out of your physical body. Each of you chose to come to this planet at this time and have an experience as a Human **Being**. Yes, you have most likely had human experiences before and that is why you can access past life experiences from the information contained in All Being and your Akashic Records.*

*The Akashic Records are the home of your soul when you are in your natural state. By accessing the Akashic Records you are able to have direct access to your soul and the Masters, Teachers and Loved Ones that guide your soul on its journey. This was why we guided you, Robin, to learn to read the Akashic Records, because of your ability to see the bigger picture of All Being and how each soul is an integral part of the whole and yet each soul is the whole because we are All Being all the time.*

*Ok, that was a mouthful! We know this is a difficult concept and we would ask you, Robin, to remember that it took a year of study with Creatious—a channeled Being of Light—for you and your classmates to truly get this concept. I think it would be a great time for you to share your story of your fear of the projected outcomes for the year 2012 with your readers.*

**Robin:** In the year that I spent in class with Creatious, we spent a lot of time talking about Earth changes and projections about what could happen during this time of shift on the planet, which was emphasized by the Mayan Calendar's ending on December 21, 2012 and other prophesizes of other great cultures for this timeframe.

In our classes, Creatious shared with us how the Earth would be shifting, requiring her to free herself of structures in the way of her natural pathways and to cleanse herself of the poisons that mankind has so thoughtlessly spilled onto and into her.

Needless to say, I was developing a great sense of fear in my physical body, even though intellectually I knew what Creatious meant and I understood the concept of "we don't die, we just shed our physical body." In any case, I was really scared. I was scared for my family and friends that I loved. I was scared that my family would leave the planet and I would not. I was scared that I would leave the planet and my family would not. My fear was out of control and I needed help. At the end of this chapter, I will share with you the meditation that Yeshua shared with me to live my life fully without the fear of death.

This period of my life taught me that our experience in our human bodies is very temporary and that we need to appreciate our family and friends and honor our cosmically brief time with them. I work very hard to be in the present moment with my family, my friends and my clients, too. Every moment that we are here in our human body is a gift to experience all that life can offer us. Honor this time, for we may never pass this way again.

**Robin:** Yeshua, why did these teens have to die so tragically?

*Yeshua: Let's expand this to the category of all children. Death is not random. Before you enter your physical body, your soul knows when it is going to leave the physical body. Therefore, these children were not consciously aware of their impending death on the physical level but they were aware of it on the soul level. All souls come into this lifetime with a purpose and some will achieve their goals and others will not. Some will be here for a very short time and other will live a long life.*

*The more unusual or tragic a person's passing, the more we take notice and the more we are motivated to change the status quo—and the more we are motivated to find a cure for a disease, to change teen driving laws, to change laws about texting and driving, to require greater restrictions on what we can bring onto an airplane, and the more we take a stand against our perceived negative behavior or that of another person or group of people. Do you see the pattern? Tragedy is an impetus for great change. Parents have done amazing work in honor of their deceased children, towns have come together to support their local families in time of need, nations have rallied together to assist earthquake-torn countries. We are sorry that it hurts so much, but how you react to the suffering is also part of the experience. Will you wallow in your misery or will you find ways to make positive changes?*

*If we expand this concept to say that not only did these children know when they were leaving the planet on a soul level but they also chose their parents, does that mean that those parents chose a life of suffering? Of course not. They chose a life of potential greatness because the deaths of their children could springboard them into making significant differences in the lives of other children and their parents. As we have stated before, we never give you experiences that you cannot handle. It may take a lifetime to understand, but you will—whether in physical or non-physical form—we can promise you that.*

**Robin:** Did HaShem actually think the Jews could handle the Holocaust and all of the other atrocities that the Jews have been subjected to?

*Yeshua: In a big way, YES. I know that this is a very sensitive subject and I will try to explain this in the best way that I can. I ask that you hear this with an open heart, Robin; we can feel your pain around this subject. Earlier in the book, we explained that if we are open to seeing the world through other people's perspectives, we can accept their point of view without judgment. We also explained that you do not need to condone or agree with their behavior.*

*Mass genocide is not an acceptable behavior on your planet, period. That is in complete contradiction to the teachings of God. The Holocaust had many victims of genocide but the Jews were included in this important teaching to mankind because of their deep faith in God. The lesson—that mass genocide is not acceptable under any circumstances—is now a part of the fabric of mankind, especially because the Jews will not let mankind ever forget what happened. By keeping these tragic events in everyone's conscious mind, this important teaching of God will continue. So, yes, we still have mass genocide on the planet, but the Jews are working hard to keep it from slipping away from the consciousness of mankind. We will never get to a state of planetary Oneness, as long as mass genocide still exists anywhere.*

**Robin:** Now, I'm just a bit confused. Earlier you asked the Jews to let go of their persecution complex and now you are asking us to keep talking about what happened in the Holocaust. By virtue of our "never forget" agenda, how are we in accordance with the Law of Attraction? Aren't we continuing to attract persecution through our thoughts, actions and deeds related to our remembrance of the Holocaust?

*Yeshua: That is not what the Jews are doing at all. By honoring your murdered loved ones, who died so tragically, and by calling attention to the wrongness of this act and by declaring "Never Again!" you are actually working towards manifesting the "Never Again!" You have set your intentions very clearly and, as a committed group of people on the planet, you are working to ensure this will never happen to anyone again. And we applaud every moment of everyone's dedication to this proclamation.*

*But here is the kicker: mankind can never have Oneness on the planet from a defensive position. For the Jews, this means that when they can truly believe and know that by entrusting in Oneness (by putting down their swords and shields) true peace will come to the planet. And only then will the words "Never Again!" be realized. Until then, the Jewish people are just trying to prevent being persecuted once more. Let me be clear that it takes the same effort from the Muslim, Christian and all other religious communities to put down their swords and their shields. We are working diligently on them as well through other Spiritual Messengers, we promise you that.*

**Robin:** Thank you, Yeshua. Shalom for now!

## Step 6—A Practical Guide: Live your life fully, without the fear of death

1. Prepare yourself for meditation in whatever way works best for you.
2. Relax and begin to feel the connection with your heart center and the deep love that is present from your Spiritual Support Team.
3. In your deep state of sensing the vast love of your heart center, begin to imagine your dearest family and friends with you in your heart center. In your meditation, they are indeed out of their physical body and in their energetic state.
4. Ask yourself, "Now that they are all out of their physical bodies, how will I recognize each one of them?" In essence, could you recognize their energy signatures?
5. The answer is "yes" because their energy signature is the love that you feel for them when you are in their physical presence. Their energy signature is how you feel when you hug them, kiss them, laugh with them or comfort them. Feel this now for each one of them.
6. Now, we ask you to feel the energy of All Being. The energy of All Being feels like the combination of all the love that you feel for your dearest family and friends in this deep state of unconditional love and acceptance for them.
7. Now, we ask you, "If your family shed their physical bodies and merged completely back into All Being and you did not, who would be the lucky ones?" Of course, the answer most likely for you would be "them" as it was for me.
8. And then our last question is, "Now that you know their energy signature, could you ever really be without them? If your response is "no" then you can be comforted by the knowing that the physical body is a temporary vessel and that we would be back together in our natural state in what feels like the blink of an eye.

9. Take this knowing back into your life and you will be pleasantly surprised and comforted by this sense of relief that you will never be without the ones you love.

10. Now, live your life with the knowing that we do not die, we just shed our physical bodies and return to our natural state of All Being.

# *Step Seven*

*Allow your Spiritual Support Team to lead the way*

After I arrived home from India and settled into my life again, I began to think about how I would use all of this knowledge I learned at the Oneness University and my ability to now be a conduit for the Oneness Blessing (Deeksha) energy transfer. The business person in me wanted to see a return on my investment in India. Today, I can chuckle because there was never going to be a direct return on investment from my visit to the Oneness University; it would just have an impact on every single moment of my life since!

Off I went to find the perfect office space. What did I need? Maybe a healing room, a reception area and, if lucky, a small workshop space? In my research, I discovered an interesting location in Bloomfield, Connecticut. As we walked into this very large space (an entire floor of an office building), I heard my spiritual guidance say, "Welcome to your first venue." I responded, "I don't want a venue, I just want an office." My guidance responded back, "If you give us six weeks without fear, we will open this venue for you."

I showed the space to a few trusted advisors and Ori, and I agreed to sign the lease. I asked my spiritual guidance for assistance on the name of the space. While I was in a meditative state, they said "The Enlightened Professional Center" or EPiCenter for short, the central location for the spiritual community in our area. We now had a name and Spirit was busy making all the contractors come on time and all the pieces fall into place as they promised, if I showed no fear. The space was huge, with lots of wall space and lots of open rooms. A friend gave us a wonderful suggestion to invite the Spiritual Art Community to come and hang their pictures in the space like an art gallery. We put the word out to the community and the artwork came flooding in. Another friend became the Art Manager and, lo and behold, we received the perfect number of pieces of art to cover all of our walls!

Another friend and colleague came on board to assist with marketing and event production. We planned a series of grand opening events and we were ready to open. We created a beautiful, sacred space that would be used to heal and enlighten the community. Little did I know that this would become one of the most challenging times of my career and my personal life.

I was extremely hopeful that, as in the movie, *The Field of Dreams,* if I built it they would come. We began to plan events and we would have some events that were financially successful and many that were not. We were trying to find the perfect formula. Another friend joined us to add her special energy to the mix. A side of me was trying anything and everything because I wanted to pay my financial commitments to the landlord, my team and my family. However, I was not being sufficiently selective and a lack of attendance was frustrating. I was looking for enough money just to pay my bills and obtain relief from the stress.

In accordance with the Law of Attraction, that perspective is a big no-no. The Law of Attractions says that we must ask for what we want, not what we don't want. I could not see at the time that I needed to ask for financial and emotional abundance. I could not be tied to the outcomes, and I certainly should not have limited my success to just paying my bills. I needed to be in a place of belief and allowing, but I was in neither. I was just stressed out and not happy.

In retrospect, the EPiCenter was a wonderful catalyst for bringing together the spiritual community of greater Hartford. Because of our efforts, wonderful learning and healing did take place, and people have expressed gratitude to us for that. When we decided to close the EPiCenter, we received many notes of thanks. While the community was upset with our decision, I knew it was the right one for me. I had invested a significant amount of funds in the EPiCenter and the fund was now depleted. The community was upset but I had learned what I had been guided to learn.

My two years with the EPiCenter served as an important educational opportunity for me. I was able to listen to and interact with highly regarded teachers and healers. I began to understand what it meant to be a leader in the community. I was able to discern what our business was and how I would manage it going forward. In essence, I paid for this education just like any other university but I was able to be of service to my community at the same time. It might seem almost perfect except for one major problem.

I was never home for that two-year period. My relationship with Ori was in bad shape. He kept asking me where his wife was and I kept thinking he meant corporate Robin—the successful business person. He truly meant **just me**, but I was too immersed in the EPiCenter and my own frustrations to see that. Instead of looking at his suggestions as support, I looked at them as criticism. It was tough; I needed him to be part of the EPiCenter and yet I could not hear him or accept him without inferring judgment. I asked him to step away from the business and, with that, widened the crack in our relationship. That decision set me up for a critical lesson about relationships.

## The Significance of Step 7—A Conversation with Yeshua

**Robin:** Yeshua, during this time period, I had two major issues occurring at once. The first was my lack of ability to trust in the Law of Attraction and allow abundance into my life. The second was the crack in the pavement of my relationship with Ori. We previously dedicated an entire step to the Law of Attraction and we presented the Universal Roadmap for our readers to consider. Would you like to address this once more here?

*Yeshua: Yes, I would. In your first 25 years of working, another person or system told you what your value was. Based on your*

67

*performance, you were given a certain amount of money and various office sizes and other perks. Corporate America is a well-oiled abundance machine. You had the inherent abundance system down to a science but then when you left Corporate America and you had to value your own time and your own contribution. You could not do it for a long time. We are pleased that you have finally "got it" but like many small business owners, it was a difficult journey.*

*We knew that we had to throw you into the lion's den in order to get you to see how you could attract a beautiful event space, a wonderful team of helpers and a new circle of friends and community that would come to the Enlightened Professional Center for learning and community. On one hand, you saw it and allowed us to surround you with like-minded friends and colleagues, but you were not in a place to accept all the abundance that we so graciously wanted to share with you. The sad part about this time period is that you had all the skills to make this a grand success but you did not have the confidence in your ability to manifest what you needed to support the efforts. This refusal to allow abundance and to be in a constant state of worry about not having enough money was creating the perfect storm for placing tremendous strain on every aspect of your life.*

*Do you remember that particular Sunday when Ori announced he was going kayaking and you started yelling at him from your phone in the EPiCenter? You were yelling, "I never get to have any fun, this is all work and no rewards, I hate this place." Ori told you to get off the phone and get your act together. So, you walked into your healing room and in a screaming rage, you started shouting at the picture of Sri AmmaBhaghan about how exhausted you were and you were done with this existence and that they should send you something else to do.*

*The next morning, you received a phone call from a colleague from the company that you worked at for 20 years. A job had been posted that if you had stayed at your company, you would have grown into. The Universe was sending you your perfect corporate job. Why did we do this? Because you asked for something else to do for your work with such great conviction, we sent you the opportunity. What you subsequently learned is that we sent you what you asked for, not necessarily what you truly wanted. You wanted relief and abundance within the EPiCenter, not a corporate job.*

*Attracting and allowing abundance into our lives is a difficult concept for many, especially for those in the Spiritual Arts. Why is that? Is it the vows of poverty that many of you associate with this field of work and that many clients don't think they should pay for spirituality? Why not? Just because someone works in a spiritual field they still have expenses to pay on the Earth plane. It is important to always ask for a fair exchange of energy, with money being the prevalent form of energy exchange for work.*

**Robin:** The second big opportunity for growth during this time period was my relationship with Ori. I needed Ori's support so much then and yet I took every word he said to me as criticism.

*Yeshua: Yes, you both were having a tough time in your relationship and you were introduced to "The Power of TED" (by David Emerald), an interesting perspective on working and personal relationship. You both read the book and it made a dramatic impact on your relationship. Central to the shift is a transformation in mindset from a Victim Orientation to a Creator Orientation. The bottom line for you and Ori was that every time he gave you a suggestion, you were in the role of Victim and you saw him either as the Persecutor or Rescuer. And to make matters even worse, he was doing the same thing as you tried to coach him at this time.*

*For, you see, Ori was also anxious to step onto his spiritual journey but he could not find the right place to begin. Once you both began to shift from Victim to Creator and then saw each other's suggestions as either Challenger (vs. Persecutor) or Coach (vs. Rescuer), your entire relationship shifted. You began to see the innate wisdom and experience that you both had admired in each other for almost twenty years. This was a very important shift as Ori would now begin to step onto his spiritual path and you would take the experience received from your time at the EPiCenter and move into the most challenging part of your journey to your Messiah Within.*

**Robin:** I keep thinking about the crack in the pavement of our relationship at that time and how that pertains to marriage in general today. It takes such a deep commitment to maintain a marriage in today's world environment. It feels like the entire Universe conspires to make marriages not work. For 50% of the population of married couples, they give up and get divorced. For the other 50%, it takes a tremendous desire, commitment and constant action to make the relationship continue to work.

*Yeshua: Let's explore the Judaic perspective on marriage. "A man who does not marry is not a complete person." (Lev. 34a) "Any man who has no wife lives without joy, without blessing, and without goodness." (B. Yev. 62b). Judaism views marriage as a holy sanctification of life and as the fulfillment of God's commandment. The Ketubah is the marriage contract that has protected the sanctity of marriage and the stability of the Jewish family.*

*Think back, Robin, to when you were starting to date young men and how important it was for your parents that you dated Jewish men and how important it was to marry a Jewish man. This was part of the fabric of your Jewish heritage, part of the desire to survive. This desire is deeply woven into the persecution complex that we chatted about before. The Jews are survivors and Judaism is an integral part of the fabric of our world culture.*

*However, we see a unique opportunity for the Jews to open up to the concept of Oneness and expand their perspective to a world view and acceptance without judgment of other world religions and cultures. This is important for the next generations of Jews who have for the past 30 years been born with an inner compass toward Oneness. How can we expect them to continue to embrace any religion that does not embrace all mankind?*

*Yes, it is so much easier to be in a marriage where the two partners have similar life experiences, where they can share the customs and family heritage. But Judaism and other world religions must expand and grow in tolerance to meet the next generations where they are in regard to unlimited tolerance. This is why we see so much inter-marriage and an apparent disregard for this notion of marrying within your own religion by our young people. They would much rather marry someone who embraces their world or overall spiritual view than someone who embraces their parents' religious view. How can mankind improve this? The answer will be critical to the survival of all religions.*

*For you and Ori, you have lived multiple lifetimes as husband and wife and, therefore, you bring forward a strong history of Jewish and other cultural survival. However, your challenges as a couple are unique and we will explore them going forward in the chapters ahead. Stay tuned!*

**Robin:** Thank you, Yeshua. Shalom for now!

**Step 7—A Practical Guide: Allow your Spiritual Support Team to lead the way**

1. Once again, find a quiet space for you to be in conversation with your Spiritual Support Team or your internal guidance system; they are one and the same.

2. If you are noticing a pattern, you are correct: it is very important to become quiet so you can hear your internal guidance. Turn off all the distracting elements and become quiet. When and where is up to you.

3. Begin the conversation by expressing gratitude for this opportunity to speak with your Spiritual Support Team.

4. Surrender to the knowing that your internal guidance system will always provide you with direction that is in your highest and best good.

5. Ask how you can be of greatest service to mankind.

6. Be open to hearing the answer, no matter how logical or illogical it sounds right now. Sometimes we will hear a small part of a plan or a hint of a grander plan that takes work in both the internal and external world to give it greater formulation.

7. Express gratitude for the information received and ask to be shown in your awake state the people who can assist you and be provided with the resources to achieve the steps shown to you on your life's path.

8. Move forward without FEAR of the unknown.

9. Watch in awe of the synchronistic events that begin to occur in your life that enable you to fulfill your greatest desires.

10. As you become aware of and express gratitude for the synchronistic events in your life, the more you will see them and the easier it will become to react to them. For, you see, they are always occurring—you may be just too busy to notice. Slow your life down so you can notice them!

# *Step Eight*

*Be open to learning all lessons placed on your path*

In August of 2008, I travelled to California to attend a Oneness University sponsored event with my Oneness friends. In attendance were more than 200 Oneness Blessing Givers and a Senior Teacher from the University. The theme of the seminar was learning to become an *Agent of Suffering*. The concept was that if we could face situations head on that create suffering opportunities in our lives and if we could learn to honor them and live them, then at the end of the suffering we would have the greatest gifts we could imagine—the joy we so richly deserved. I laughed to myself and said, "Sri AmmaBhagavhan, who would ever want to suffer on purpose? Not me!"

I turned to my friend with whom I went to India with to say "Are you kidding me—I won't do that." But what happened when I turned to look at him was beyond anything I could have possibly imagined. I was being shown by Sri AmmaBhagavhan my Twin Flame—the yang to my yin—my spiritual equal. Instead of being thrilled for this discovery, I was devastated. While Ori and I were on a bumpy road in our marriage, somehow our commitment to each other was as strong as ever. Thank goodness, my friend had the same level of personal integrity as Ori and I knew that I was safe with my friend to go through this process of suffering. Little did I realize the suffering would last more than two years.

The Twin Flame relationship is an interesting spiritual concept. When two people are on their spiritual journey, the Divine may show them their Twin Flame and give them the opportunity to do great work together that is spiritual in nature and will benefit the greater consciousness. In essence, the person who enters your life is the twin of your soul. This relationship generates great love but not in the traditional sense of the word. The love is Divine and is intended to be used in service to mankind.

If you are blessed to meet your Twin Flame, you will meet a person who reflects back to you your own Divine light. When you look at this person, you see reflected back to you the love that you are. It is not intended for a traditional relationship. In fact, to be in a traditional relationship with your Twin Flame would require you to look into the eyes of your own divinity every day and would require two very deeply committed individuals to pursue this type of relationship. It was very clear that neither my friend nor I wanted that. I was deeply committed to Ori and my children and my friend was deeply committed to his independence and freedom to live his spiritual life.

What my friend and I had to do was much harder than a traditional relationship. My friend's job as my Twin Flame was to expose the pearl that was my golden heart and to give me the courage and vision to become my own *Messiah Within*. My job as my friend's Twin Flame was to show him how he was unconditional love and to honor that aspect in him so that he would be ready to be in a more traditional relationship with someone else. And my friend was true to his task; he kept rubbing my heart trying to expose the pearl and it was raw for two years. I was true to my task, by honoring and showing him what true commitment was in my relationship to Ori.

It is very easy now to write this from a place of retrospect but, oh my, the journey was difficult and painful. For those two years, I remained deeply and passionately in love with my husband but I was also given a directive from the Divine to reflect back to my Twin Flame the love that he was. My heart felt like it was split in half—one half to Ori and the other half to my Twin Flame, to help him on his journey. Throughout this entire period, my Twin Flame would sweetly refer to me as Mrs. Clare as a gentle reminder of the true priority in my life, Ori.

In my meditations, in my periods of great suffering, I would hear Sri AmmaBhagavhan saying to me, "Live every day, Feel every emotion, Honor every opportunity to learn. Just continue to be unconditional love no matter how much it hurts. We promise a glorious outcome if you do." And I would respond, "I just want to be One with the Divine—why can't I have this instead of this painful existence?" It was like my soul knew the answer but my heart was not reaching this same conclusion because my heart was living the experience from a dysfunctional state.

Intellectually and spiritually, I understood the task before me and all of our respective roles, but emotionally I had some serious work to do. I remember feeling like I was working at the maturity level of a teenager, not the mature spiritual woman that I was. Little did I know at the time that I was seeing this through my teen heart, due to a deep emotional scar that needed to be healed. By bringing my heart down to its rawest state, I was shown that my heart was shattered into many pieces and I had given away pieces of my heart to many people in my life who loved me. I would learn that in order to become my Messiah Within, I must have my whole heart intact, so that I could fully embrace my own inner divinity. This process took place over three unique healing opportunities in three sacred locations in my life.

## The Significance of Step 8—A Conversation with Yeshua

**Robin:** It is now time to write about the Twin Flame relationship and I am finding this so difficult to do. I thought that since I had written about it for a local magazine, then it would be easier to write now. But it is not and I guess I'm wondering why. My life has moved on and my world is calmer and more peaceful and yet, when I think of this time, I am still so sad. Can you help me to understand?

*Yeshua: Robin, we feel your tears about this time and we want you to know that it is actually a lot simpler than you make it. We placed you in the middle of a great love story and that was the process of falling in love with yourself. We just placed beautiful souls like Ori and your Twin Flame in the way to awaken your heart. But your true heart belongs to God or All Being and we know that you know that. Even in the midst of all the pain above, you would call out to us to only have to love us and we answered you.*

*At the time, you thought you were asking us for relief from the torture of living your life with your heart torn in half. But do you see it now? We had to saw your heart in half, energetically, so you could let us in to reach your greatest knowing, your Messiah Within. This took a great more work and we will explain further in the next few chapters. But at this stage of the process, we had to open the door and both of these men played a huge role in this.*

*Ori was to provide you with a sense of safety and security and arms that you could fall into and rest. The readers might be thinking that you had an affair—if not physical, then with the heart. We are here to confirm, Robin, that you did not have an affair—at least how it is defined as part of your social norms. This was **sacred** work—plain and simple.*

*Ori and your Twin Flame are both ancient souls just like you and they have both been through these times themselves in their spiritual development. But, Robin, think also how much you influenced their lives by giving them your heart. Do you even comprehend the depth of a heart that is on the path to Oneness with the Divine? Please think about this. You gave your heart to so many people in this time period: your beautiful children, your family and friends, the customers and clients of the EPiCenter. The love you gave them was no greater or less than the love you gave to Ori and your Twin Flame.*

*When we love each person unconditionally regardless of their status in our lives, then we have reached a state of Oneness. You loved your Twin Flame unconditionally—meaning that you accepted him without judgment. Do you recall that he would say to you, "You never see the earthly me—your perception of me is unrealistic. If you truly knew me, you would not like me that much." But don't let the earthly Twin Flame fool you; the spiritual Twin Flame adored that you saw him at the core of his soul.*

*Can you imagine how hard it was for him to say goodbye to you? What man would not want to be adored? But you did your job well, Robin. He felt adored enough to move onto a relationship with a lovely woman that is a good match for him in both the physical and the spiritual path. We know that you miss him, but one day you will be friends again, we promise. For now, he is focusing his attention on his new love and you are focusing your attention on your life with Ori.*

*Let's discuss Ori during this time frame. Think about what it took for him to give you the freedom to explore this time in your life. We worked very closely with him, helping him to release any feelings of jealousy and resentment. At the same time, he could see your distress and he could see how much you loved him and how you were not willing to let go. That, my friend, was enough for him at the time. He truly loves you unconditionally and he always has. He has loved you for so many lifetimes, some that were lovely and some that were very difficult. But for the most part, in all of them he has been just the way he is in this lifetime—loving you with all of his heart.*

*And last, but certainly not least, let's talk about Robin in this period. This was a perfect example of surrender. I see you smiling—okay, perhaps you went kicking and screaming, but you truly surrendered to your spiritual path. Do you see that? For all of you, we are sorry to say that this path is not always going to be paved in roses. But the real question is, how much do you have to suffer on the path?*

*Let's talk about the request from Sri AmmaBhagavhan to become "An Agent of Suffering." What does that truly mean? If you ask five people, you will get five different answers. Here is my answer: life itself will provide us with many opportunities to suffer but do we have to truly suffer through them? No. Suffering is a state of mind only. Therefore, will the cycle of life provide us with opportunities to be sad, mad, fearful, frustrated? Of course, but do we have to suffer?*

*Only if we choose to. In the twelve-step program for individuals with addictive behaviors there is a saying, "Let Go, Let God." That is a profound statement of how to live your life without suffering. We can accept that opportunities to learn and grow will be provided to us, but we do not have to suffer.*

*What if we looked at our own lives the way we look at other people's lives? In our greatest moments of compassion, we can feel their sorrow and we can express our compassion through acts of Gemilut Chassidim, or acts of loving kindness, but we cannot suffer for them. What if we looked at our own lives in this manner? What if we were the loving observer of our own lives? We would face ourselves with an open heart, asking "What can I do to help you? What kindness can I show you today?" We would approach our problem with the grace of knowing that through self-kindness and, of course, surrendering the problem to your Spiritual Support Team, you can resolve the problem in a way that feels kinder and gentler.*

**Robin:** Thank you, Yeshua. Shalom for now!

## Step 8—A Practical Guide: Be open to learning all lessons placed on your path

1. Gather around you an earthly Spiritual Support Team— friends, family, spiritual professionals to be your sounding board.
2. Be open to living each lesson placed on your path.
3. Do not run and hide from this process with coping mechanisms.
4. Feel and honor the pain of each lesson.
5. Engage in conversation with your earthly support team.
6. Stick with it. We promise that the insights you gain will far outweigh the pain of living through the lessons.
7. Step outside, ask Mother Earth for her loving support. Walk, look at the stars, feel the energy of the trees. Know that you are not alone on this journey.
8. Write in your journal; write a letter to your Divine source asking him/her for the meaning of these lessons.
9. Be quiet so you can hear the answers. Be amazed at the simplicity of the answers.
10. Implement the answers learned from the lessons in your life as you move one step closer to true happiness.

# *Step Nine*

*Return your heart to a state of emotional*
*and energetic wholeness*

The first part of this time period I call "mending my shattered heart" occurred in a sacred place in my life—our family home in Pennsylvania. I was awakened by my spiritual guidance to journal. This happened a lot during this two-year period. I needed to write in order to feel sane. I would start each letter "Dear HaShem" and then spill my guts over what I was feeling. This ritual helped release the steam from the valve of my intense emotional state. On this particular night, my Spiritual guidance helped me to see that my heart was actually shattered into many small pieces, and showed me who had all the pieces of my heart. If I was to heal completely, I must get them back. But how would I do that?

Within the next two months, I was guided to visit a sacred spot in Gloucester, Massachusetts called Good Harbor Beach. I went to walk on Good Harbor Beach in March and I knew that the answers could only be found there. As I left my room at the inn, I encountered the most magnificent sunrise over the small island near the beach. It was one of the most spectacular sites I had ever seen. I was so enthralled that I started to cry. And then I kept on crying . . . I was still weeping after one hour on the beach. I decided that I could not go back to the inn so I crawled up into the dunes to hide. Many dogs were running free on the beach at that time of year, and they kept coming to check on me, but I promised them I was okay.

It was time for part two. I was told that I had to forgive and release the person who shattered my heart, which created all the small pieces that I would subsequently give away. I knew that was my college love, so I cried and released the karmic ties into the ocean. I made my way back to the inn and back to my home. I listened to my voicemails and heard my sister-in-law's message that my college love was trying to reach me and she took his number for me. I looked up at the sky and said "I have to talk to him after 30 years of holding this heartbreak? Haven't I been tortured enough?"

I called him and he said the most amazing thing. "I live on the beach in Florida and I was walking early this morning and all of a sudden I thought you had died and I had to find out." He must have felt the karmic ties being cut by Spirit on our behalf. My response to him was, "How spiritual are you? Because what I have to say will require an open mind." We chatted, we got re-acquainted, and we both apologized for our parts in our mutually broken hearts. My college love wanted to see me face-to-face to reminisce, but I felt I was not able to do so. I was going through enough in my life at the time.

My heart felt like it was exploding from all the healing and all the emotions. I began to feel depressed. One day, I felt like not getting out of bed ever again. I actually got angry and said "I am not this person—this ends now." I jumped into my meditation chair and I said, "I will not leave here until I feel better!" Then part three began. I went into a deep meditation and two Ascended Masters came into my bedroom—Yeshua ben Yosef and Moses.

I was in AWE to see them standing in front of me. Yeshua poured a substance down into my throat chakra—it was cool and numbing. I thought, "This feels nice" and it relaxed me. For what was to come next was not very pleasant—Yeshua and Moses each reached one hand into my heart chakra and pulled off the grey mass/shield that was covering my heart. I cried in pain and said out loud, "This hurts so much but please don't stop" and they did not. They finished and I bowed my head in reverence to them and they disappeared.

Now that the energetic casing was removed from my heart and it was truly exposed, it was time for a ceremony to return my heart to its completeness. Another Divine being came forward and worked with me to have all the people (in an energetic, not physical form) return the pieces of my heart to me that I had given away. I was able energetically to express my gratitude and ask for or give forgiveness as needed to each energetic body that came forth. The Divine Being held all the pieces for me until the procession was complete. Then, together, we took a golden thread and tied my heart together until it was 99% whole. For, you see, there was one energetic being whose piece of my heart I was unable to accept, and that was my Twin Flame. Unfortunately, we were not done yet with our work. That would take a bit more time, as well as a conversation with Ori.

## The Significance of Step 9—A Conversation with Yeshua

**Robin:** It seemed like every moment of my life at this time was chock full of spiritual opportunity. It was like I was on a treasure hunt and the treasure was my own inner divinity. As the readers can see, many growth opportunities occurred for me at this time. I could ask you a hundred questions and yet I can't seem to think of a single one. Why is that?

*Yeshua: Yes, my dear one, there were many lessons learned and many opportunities to grow and what you are struggling with is how to discern which were the most important. All of them were of equal importance and I will summarize for you what we had in mind for you during that time frame.*

*Have you noticed, Robin, that we always give great teachings in steps? Even within a step are lots of steps! We do that so we don't scare any of you away from finding your own treasure or your own inner divinity. Many of you are conscientiously moving along on your spiritual journeys because you can see with each step comes a profound learning. This takes patience and a natural state of curiosity.*

*When your heart was shattered energetically in college, you began to give it away with each subsequent relationship, romantic or otherwise. This was creating a void in your energetic field where your full heart needed to be. We needed to bring in your Twin Flame to help expose the pearl of your beautiful heart. Once he completed his task, we then needed to work with you to understand how depleted you were energetically and to provide you the tools to bring back all the pieces of your heart.*

*But one other important aspect is the work that Moses and I did to remove the grey mass. The grey mass was a shield that you had energetically put on to protect what was left of your heart. This shield was a tool that you created to ensure that your heart would never be shattered again. In many of your requests at this time, you would cry out to be in Oneness with us. However, the grey shield was preventing us from reaching your heart and you were not truly letting us in because you were afraid of the pain. In your mind, you knew that we could never hurt you, but this shield was thirty years in the making. Of course, you have experienced great love during those thirty years—your husband, your children, your family and friends, and your dog, Hailey. But to reach your greatest desire—Oneness with All Being—your heart had to become whole and you could only do that with the shield removed.*

**Robin:** I find it interesting that I am writing about forgiveness on Yom Kippur or the Day of Atonement. You would think by now that coincidences wouldn't faze me but I am always so intrigued by them and this one is no exception. Can we talk about forgiveness and the importance of it on our journey?

**Yeshua:** *Currently, you are in the month of Elul or the time of repentance on the Jewish calendar. The name of the month is an acronym for the "Ani l'dodi v'dodi li" or "I am my Beloved's and my Beloved is mine," a quote from Song of Songs 6:3, where the Beloved is God and the "I" is the Jewish people. Your readers would be interested to know that Ori wears a pendant on his neck with these words, which he attributes to his love for you. But beyond* *the perceived coincidence of the necklace, the words, "I am my Beloved's and my Beloved is mine" can be misinterpreted to sound like a possession.*

*These are actually great words of Oneness because in these words are an act of great surrender and connection. Therefore, during Elul we try to further enhance the Oneness created between mankind and HaShem by forgiving each other and living the attributes previously defined as bringing Heaven to Earth. If we can live the Divine attributes on the Earth plane, then we have achieved HaShem's purpose for mankind.*

*In Aramaic, the word "Elul" means "search," and during this time of the year, many Jewish people will search their hearts for the ability to ask for forgiveness and to receive forgiveness. Elul is the time that we truly ask forgiveness of others. As you read in the text in synagogue, HaShem cannot forgive us for sins committed against another person until we have first obtained forgiveness from the person we have wronged.*

*I know you also struggle with the concept that HaShem will not forgive us until we do "anything that is written in the religious text" because you know there is no judgment from All Being, only acceptance. The ancient religious texts were written to give people a goal to reach for, not a destination. The purpose of the text was to say to mankind, "reach towards an ideal relationship with God" and the achievement of that goal was the pinnacle point of life for many. I am here to say that the goal is still the same, except that God is not something we reach for on the outside but within our internal being. God is not out there, up there or anywhere in particular—God is everywhere, which would logically enable us to say that God is within you.*

**Robin:** Thank you, Yeshua. Shalom for now!

## Step 9—A Practical Guide: Return your heart to a state of emotional and energetic wholeness

1. Determine if you heart is in a state of emotional and energetic wholeness.
2. How do you know if your heart is energetically whole? The answer lies in your ability to maintain a consistent feeling of Oneness in your life.
3. Once again, find that quiet, peaceful place in your life so that you may hear or work with your Spiritual Support Team.
4. Bring yourself into a deep meditation.
5. Request that a member of your Spiritual Support Team (either one that is alive or in spirit) come to assist you.
6. With the help of this guide, request that the energetic signature of all folks whom you wish to receive or give forgiveness to come forward in your meditation.
7. One by one, extend and receive forgiveness and ask for the piece of your heart they are holding onto.
8. Express gratitude to each of these people for participating in this ceremony today.
9. Once all the pieces are in place, work with your Spiritual Support Team to sew together the pieces of your energetic heart with an energetic golden thread that will be provided by HaShem.
10. When the heart is completely sewn together, return from your deep meditation and rest. (As simple as the request to rest sounds, this is emotionally charged work and you will need time to acclimate to your new whole heart. The more full and whole your heart is, the greater the energy of All Being you can carry in your heart. Please do not underestimate the importance of rest.)

# *Step Ten*

*Live your life in the present moment without regret of
the past or fear of the future*

At times, when I was frustrated with my own suffering, I would
try to blame Ori and would speak poorly of him to my girlfriends.
What I realized is that the more I talked about the negative aspects
of our relationship, the more I received negativity in our relationship.
Another Law of Attraction example—the Universe was delivering to
me exactly what I was thinking and speaking about!

We were with my extended family during Thanksgiving and
everyone kept saying to me, "Wow, Ori is really spiritual now." I
would be thinking, "Ori who?" I was caught up in finding someone
to blame for my misery. But in a moment of reflection, I began to see
what my family was talking about. I decided to tell my girlfriends
only positive things about Ori, and guess what? Our relationship
became much more positive.

Ori was now more deeply committed to his own spiritual journey,
which combined Judaism and Shamanism. Because of his opening
to his spiritual gifts, we began to grow closer on a spiritual level
and I was finding the role that my Twin Flame played in my life was
diminishing. Could Ori and I have it all? Could we be both Earth
mates and spiritual mates? Could this be one of the gifts that Sri
AmmaBhagavhan had promised me? Only time would tell.

During the summer of 2010, Ori and I returned to Good Harbor
Beach for a summer get-away. It was on this vacation that I began
to channel the Divine realm and I was able to share with Ori great
insights about his spiritual journey. We loved our time together.
We awoke one morning to a great fog on the beach, so thick that

you could not see a foot in front of you. My spiritual guidance said, "Please ask Ori to go for a walk." So, I did and he said, "Yes."

We stepped onto the beach and my spiritual guidance said, "Tell Ori about your Twin Flame—the whole story." I said, "I can't, I'm afraid." They said, "See the fog around you? That is us, both of your spiritual guides, your deceased loved ones and the angelic realm. Today is the day, you are both ready." So, I said, "Ori, I have something to tell you" and I began the story. When I finished the story, I could not believe it, we were out on the island. We had walked out to the island, it was low tide, and there was not a drop of water between the island and the beach. Neither of us had ever seen that before.

When I finished the story, Ori looked me in the eyes and said, "Did you learn the lessons that Sri AmmaBhagavhan asked you to learn that day in California?" I said, "Yes" and he responded, "Isn't that all that really matters?" I stood there in disbelief. I was waiting for him to yell and be angry, but he was not at all. He turned and walked away to explore the island, and I prayed to the Divine for extending to us such grace and for my blessing in Ori. He returned to me and I went to give him the Oneness Blessing. I collapsed in his arms asking for forgiveness. He said, "There is nothing to forgive, Robin. You did nothing wrong and I love you unconditionally." I knew then and there that I was exactly where I was supposed to be, in the arms of the man who loved me unconditionally. He always had and he always would. I was so deeply blessed.

The message I received from my inner guidance was so simple. *In the present moment, what do I truly know for sure about my husband, about myself and about our relationship*? Not what happened in the past or what I feared what could happen in the future but right now, right this very moment. What did I know for sure? The answer was clear—*my life was perfect and just as it should be*. When I removed the regrets of the past and the fear of the future, I was present in the knowing of the unconditional love, commitment, safety and integrity that my marriage is based on. It was from the place of living in the present moment and gratitude for what we share that we continued our relationship and our spiritual studies.

I could now ask for the last piece of my heart back from my Twin Flame. The lessons had been learned on my end and I prayed the same for him. I could now sew back in the last remaining piece of my heart with the golden thread to make it whole. Now, my whole heart was a warm, loving, peaceful place for my Messiah to reside within. I could now access the most sacred answers to life's deeper meaning and be of greater service to my family, friends, clients and anyone else who would like to listen. People who know me well say I am more peaceful and my new friends say I look like I know something important. Yes, I would say that both are true; I am peaceful in the knowing that my life became simpler when I began to access and value the wisdom of my Messiah Within. I wish this same knowing for you.

## The Significance of Step 10—
## A Conversation with Yeshua

**Robin:** I have never experienced such grace as the time on Good Harbor Beach with Ori. Thank you for believing in us and for supporting us as we talked and listened during this important time in our relationship. It was as if the veil between the spiritual and the physical realms dissolved in order to place us in a cocoon of Oneness. Ori and I became One that day in our conversation. We also became One with our Spiritual Support Team and with the Earth's elements—the sand, the island, the water, the fog. It was as if we accomplished what you have referred to as bringing Heaven to Earth. We were everywhere at once, we were in fact in All Being and yet, we were just two married people walking on the beach.

HaShem set us up with the perfect scenario to see each other in our most vulnerable truths and to see the great love we shared and to honor our individual and mutual connection to the Divine. I was just about to write, if I am never given another gift of this caliber again that will be alright. But I would be missing the point of all of this and that is that what happened on Good Harbor Beach between Ori and me can be our ongoing way of life if we choose the path to our Messiah Within. It is in our recognition that we are One with All that all miracles in our lives are possible. Am I correct?

*Yeshua: Yes, you are correct. It was our pleasure to show you what life will be like when the Messiah Consciousness moves from the extraordinary to the ordinary on planet Earth.*

**Robin:** There is a famous quote about living in the present moment, "The past is a good place to visit but I would not want to live there." I have felt like that in the process of writing this book. I have had to dive into the past with great retrospection and sometimes it was hard to write in the past and live in the present moment. What is the value of reviewing the past so intensely on our spiritual journeys?

*Yeshua: The traditional purpose of reviewing your past is to identify positive or negative patterns that you may wish to continue or give up if they do not serve you any longer. For the purposes of this book and for this time of great shift, there is an additional element and that is the discovery of a path to greater spiritual understanding and commitment. It truly is no different than learning to do anything well from your educational studies to learning to play the piano. Every lesson builds on the next. It is in the understanding of the lessons in the order received that you begin to build confidence in your abilities.*

*Your spiritual path happens whether you are paying attention or not. Many of your readers will say, "I'm not a spiritual person, this does not apply to me." But that simply cannot be true if your spiritual path is constantly unfolding before you. Whether you are open to receiving and understanding the lessons on your path is entirely up to you. You can live your life on a "day-to-day" basis, in a form of existence that has regrets from the past or fears of the future, or you can have an extraordinary life. An extraordinary life takes a commitment to working in tandem with your Spiritual Support Team. How can you help them to help you? You can do this by being clear about what you want in your life and being open to receiving their guidance. In your life, Robin, we asked you to identify four criteria for making a decision; can you share these criteria as the practical guide for this section of the book?*

**Robin:** Of course, I would be delighted to. Thank you, Yeshua. Shalom for now!

## Step 10—A Practical Guide: Criteria for making any decision in Robin's personal or work life

1. Will this action that I am deciding upon enable me to be of further service to my fellow man, the Earth and all of her inhabitants?

2. Will this action that I am deciding upon enable me to have greater joy in my life?

3. Will this action that I am deciding upon bring more peace to my family and me?

4. Will this action that I am deciding upon generate more abundant resources for all parties involved in this action?

5. If you are satisfied with the responses to all four questions above, by all means move forward.

6. If you are not satisfied with all the responses, it does not mean you should not move forward with your decision but you should enter into a process of discernment that allows you to weigh the responses in relationship to their importance in the decision making process.

7. By establishing a solid set of decision criteria, you also engage your Spiritual Support Team in the process of attracting the elements of the criteria. For example, if you are clear that this action will bring you greater joy, not only are you placing your Spiritual Support Team on notice that you are looking for more joy but, most importantly, you are in a state of allowing the joy to enter into your life.

8. Visualize yourself living the results of your impending action.

9. Express gratitude for the benefits received from living the results of your impending action.

10. Allow all the benefits of your action to be received with grace.

# *Step Eleven*

Love deeply, unconditionally and
without the chains of emotional bondage

When I finished the last section of the book almost 14 months ago, I naively thought that I had finished the book. A spiritual teacher said to me, "No, Robin, you have not lived the ending yet and it will be quite a surprise." "Really?" I thought, "What could that be?" My mind ran through all kinds of scenarios from Ori and me living happily ever after to my Twin Flame coming back and pounding down my door and saying, "No, this is not how it was supposed to end, you are mine and I claim you." Okay, well that does sound a bit old-fashioned and sexist, but is that not what we all want to be . . . loved, claimed and taken care of?

Of course it is, but the real question is, "Why do we require someone else to fulfill that innate desire?" And, "Why do we hold our loved ones in emotional bondage in order to feel loved? In my deep reflection of these two questions, I discovered that my deepest fear was still present in my heart and that was my fear of being alone.

How could that be? I am surrounded externally and internally by a strong support team and yet I was afraid. What was I so afraid of? Was it writing this book? Would that be the catalyst for losing all the people I loved? Perhaps that was true for me, for you see it had happened once before.

In a past life regression, I was taken back to a lifetime to the plains of the United States during its early settlement. When the regression began, the Robin of then was sobbing on the floor of her little house on the prairie. My guide asked me, "What are you crying about?" and I said, "Someone died." She asked me to go to the funeral and I looked in the casket and it was Ori. I thought, "Oh, how sad, Ori died." After so many lifetimes together, I can count on the fact that we both die. But then she asked me to look beyond Ori's casket and when I did I saw five more caskets. The next one held my Twin Flame, who was my brother in that lifetime, and the next ones held my daughter, my son and my mother and father all of this lifetime.

The shock of seeing them all at once created an energy ball of grief that started in my first chakra (at the base of my spine) and worked its way up to my fifth chakra (in the middle of my throat). The wail became stuck in my throat and I thought that I was going to choke to death on my grief. But then I heard my breath coach's voice guiding me through how to breathe with my throat so full of emotion. With the breath, I let out this deep wail that filled my entire room.

When I calmed down, my guide asked me to go back to when the regression began and that was on the floor of the cabin. I picked myself up off the floor of the cabin and realized I was nine months pregnant. I brushed off my apron, closed the door, got myself up into my horse-drawn wagon and rode into town. My guide took me to one year later in that lifetime and asked me what I was doing at that moment in time.

I told her that I was looking out the window of my room, which was above the General Store, watching my 1-year-old son playing and being the delight of the townspeople who were watching him. For you see, he was unconditional love. He thought everyone was his family because we had no family left and therefore, everyone became our family.

My guide asked me to turn around in the room and I did. I saw a desk with paper on it and a writing instrument and I said, "I am a writer." She said, "Yes, you were a writer then and you are a writer today." The difference is if you tell your story today, you will not be left alone by your family.

I could have easily just interpreted this past life review as encouragement to be a writer in this life time and continue the book and left it at that. But there was more to be understood . . . my intense fear of being left alone created in that lifetime was like a "ball and chain" that connected Ori and me in this life time and it was time to remove the shackles.

I was guided to have Ori come to my healing space in my office. I was being asked to channel both of our Spiritual Support Teams to speak to us directly. Nothing like setting yourself up to be shot as the messenger, but my voice was the only voice that could deliver this message to Ori, and so I began the session.

"We must release each other from the bondage of our union" is what our Spiritual Support Team asked us to do. What the heck did that mean and how would we do that? Needless to say, that did not go over well with Ori, who is so beautifully grounded and anchored in our relationship. He said, "Does that mean that we need to leave each other?" And I was simultaneously thinking, "After all of this, it's over?" But our Spiritual Support Team was quick to respond, "We are only interested in how your relationships affect you spiritually, emotionally, physically and mentally. Our greatest desire is that you are joyful in all four of these aspects. However, we do not care how you cohabit on the Earth plane. So, if you and Ori can achieve joy in your relationship by staying together, by all means do that."

Ori and I are still married but our relationship has changed. In our prior limited perspective of marriage as a bond or bondage we were unable to give each other the freedom to fly and fulfill our destinies. When we released each other from the bondage of our union, it enabled us to begin to live the lives that we are both destined to live. Ori has begun his rabbinical training and will become a rabbi and fulfill his desire to blend Judaism, Spirituality and Energy Healing. I finished this book so that I can share it with you and become a Messenger of Divine Oneness.

Releasing the other in relationship means to release our attachment to each other but not necessarily from our physical connection to each other. That is the gift of free will that HaShem so graciously bestowed upon us. Our physical relationships are our choice. We must stay connected to each other for that is truly what Oneness is all about.

But we must do this from an anchor rooted deep within ourselves—it all begins and ends with our relationship with our Divine Source.

## The Significance of Step 11—
## A Conversation with Yeshua

**Robin:** Yeshua, I must admit that the request for Ori and me to release each other from the bondage of our union really got our attention. Can you elaborate on this important concept of Emotional Bondage?

*Yeshua: I have much wisdom to share on this topic and I would like to address it from the perspective of your personal relationships and then from the emotional bondage of the Jewish people that we have talked about quite often in this book. The first emotional bondage that I would like to address is the emotional bondage that occurs within your relationships—predominantly your partner relationships. In your current energetic state, mankind has a very dense physical state and this is called living in the third dimensional energies. This dense physical state requires mankind to be more reliant on each other. The more reliant you are on another than on yourself (and your own inner divinity), the less freedom you feel to live your life's purpose. You are not as independent as you might like to be. As we move into the fourth and fifth dimensional energies, we bring more light into our bodies. This process comes from following the steps of the Messiah Within as well as other methods to balance mind, body and spirit. This effort allows us to bring our relationships to the next level and that is when you are committed to each other but do not require a feeling of bondage. In these relationships, trust runs high and fear runs low.*

*Next, I would like to address emotional bondage as it pertains to the Jews. Enslavement is a familiar subject to the Jews as many of you have studied how we were slaves in Egypt under Pharaoh and certainly one could say that we were slaves in the concentration camps as well. Now, we are slaves to our own persecution complex. Of course, the persecution complex comes directly from our times of physical enslavement as well as all of the other lifetimes that included a direct attempt to eliminate a subset of the Jewish population. Please close your eyes and take a minute or two to envision what the world would be like for the Jewish people if we did not feel that we had to look over our shoulders or have armed guards at our High Holiday events or on our buses in Israel.*

*Each spring, we celebrate the holiday of Passover or Pesach. At this time, we celebrate our freedom from slavery. The name for "Egypt" in Hebrew is "Mitzrayim," from the Hebrew word "metzar" meaning "narrow" or "constriction." "Thus says HaShem: Let My people go—and they will serve Me." This is what Moses asked Pharaoh. But let me ask you this question: how can you truly be free to serve HaShem when you are enslaved to your own persecution? Until we can remove this energy as a people, we will never be truly free to serve HaShem to our ultimate ability. And our ultimate ability is to bring a state of world peace to mankind. Once more I say to you, "As the Chosen People, the Jews can choose World Peace." That is what HaShem wants for our planet.*

**Robin:** Thank you, Yeshua. Shalom for now!

## Step 11—A Practical Guide: Release from emotional bondage all others whom you love deeply.

1. If you are able to be in the same physical space as your loved one and he or she is open to this activity, sit in a quiet space and look into each other's eyes.

2. If you are not able to be in the same physical space as your loved one, then bring yourself to a quiet space where you can have peace and quiet and close your eyes.

3. Begin to reflect on the joy that this person has brought to your life and continues to bring to your life.

4. From the center of your heart, send out a beam of light and love to this person. Use this beam of light and love to connect you in unconditional love.

5. Either out loud or to yourself says these words, "I release **you** from the emotional bondage of our union."

6. If you are with another, please have him or her say the same.

7. Next, and most importantly, say, "I release **me** from the emotional bondage of our union."

8. It is not a requirement for the other to release you—only for you to release the other and yourself. For, you see, you only have to release yourself to gain emotional freedom in your life.

9. Either physically hug or energetically hug your loved one.

10. As you move back into your daily routine, begin to notice the lightness you feel in your relationships with a knowing that decisions can now be made in your highest and best good and that of your loved one.

# Step Twelve

*Know (not just think, feel or believe) that you are in complete Oneness with All Being*

I was asked to return to Good Harbor Beach by my Spiritual Support Team to write the ending of the book. I arrived on a Sunday in October with a new spiritual friend. We had rented a lovely apartment facing the ocean so that I could write the ending. The weather was magnificent—on this late October day it was 90 degrees and sunny. I looked out of my window at the children and adults swimming in the ocean, playing with their dogs and having fun on the beach.

I looked at them longingly and I thought to myself, "No I can't have fun, I have to write the ending of the book." At that moment, my left hand began to throb and I could not type. At first I was upset because I spent all this money on this beach view and I could not write. I called Ori and said, "My hand had given out" and he said, "Well, go and play."

My new friend and I went outside to have a glorious afternoon on the beach. It was an amazing gift from HaShem this day. We laughed, we told stories, we cried, we helped each other by giving each other spiritual and life advice. We went to supper, we hung out, I read her Akashic Records for her, she did energy healing on my hand—just a typical "spiritual play date"—and then we went to sleep.

I awoke at sunrise the next morning and my hand miraculously did not hurt. On my walk at sunrise on the second day at the beach, I watched the sun rise in a typically majestic manner on Good Harbor Beach. I stood at the edge of the beach where the light of the rising sun was shining on the water's edge and onto my face.

As I stood there, tears began streaming down my face. Between the tears, I exclaimed, "Yeshua, if I finish this book today, I truly have to say goodbye to everything that I know and love, I will be alone." Oh my gosh, had I not learned anything over the past 10 years? Was all of this work in vain? How could I be a Messenger of Divine Oneness when I still struggled with being alone? Through the majesty of this amazing sunrise, I heard Yeshua's soft laughter and voice once more.

## The Significance of Step 12—
## A Conversation with Yeshua

*Yeshua: The very concept that you have been running from, Robin, is the very concept that you have been running to. If we accept the challenge of becoming our Messiah Within, our own inner divinity, then we must be comfortable being in relationship with our self. In facing our fear of being alone, we seek opportunities to interact with our Spiritual Support Team that is leading us on our path to our Messiah Within. Our time alone becomes our most cherished time because it allows us to seek and find our greatest truth and that is that we are One with All That Is. My dearest Robin, you have spent considerable time alone over the past ten years and what did you find?*

**Robin:** I discovered the greatest relationships of my life—my relationship with my own inner divinity, with my Spiritual Support Team and with All Being. My family and my friends now serve to enhance the joy, peace and abundance that I experience on my path to my Messiah Within. My greatest knowing is that I am both alone and all one—they have always been one and the same. I am but a Divine spark of HaShem and yet I am an integral part of the fabric of All Being. I am indeed blessed to know this and I am eternally grateful.

**Robin:** Yeshua, I loved how my Spiritual Support Team put me out of commission (my hand) for one day so that I could play, laugh and enjoy life with my new friend. In retrospect, it seemed like a stall tactic so that I could wait one more day in order to wake up and live the ending of my book. The gift of that morning was something that I will never ever forget. Would you like to share your thoughts?

*Yeshua: Robin, here is the most important aspect of that morning. It is not what I said or how you understood it, but it was that you came to realize once again that life is a journey that is divinely guided. Your life has been blessed to great depths because you live your life in partnership with your Spiritual Support Team. When you first started writing this book, there was no way you could have known that you had not lived the ending. We could never have shown you steps 11 and 12 without you being in complete understanding of steps 1 through 10.*

*Life is a journey or a series of steps—always know that we are here teaching you every step of the way. We will never leave you or make it too hard for you. We promise that if you place your trust in us, then that trust will be honored by us. Will you have moments when life seems unbearable or hard? Of course, but with your faith in us, the period of suffering will be much less and the return to joy, peace and love will be faster. The times of joy, peace and love will become the everyday moments of your life, not the exceptions. "All in good time" is a lovely expression that defines our relationship with all of you. The word "All" defines the abundant resources that are available to you. In your commitment to becoming your Messiah Within, you have access to an incomparable and infinitely vast level of support for your life.*

**Robin:** Thank you, Yeshua. Shalom for now!

**Step 12—A Practical Guide: Know (not just think, feel or believe) that you are in complete Oneness with All Being**

(For this last practical guide, Yeshua would like to repeat the twelve steps to becoming Your Messiah Within. This "knowing" is the well-deserved outcome of achieving the first eleven steps and a gift for staying true to the path and accomplishing the most important work of your life.)

1. From your deepest point of stillness, find your inner voice that is whispering, "You are One with All."
2. Identify the spiritual path that is in greatest resonance with your inner knowing.
3. Become your Authentic Self.
4. Allow the Universe to provide you with what you need for your growth, alignment and well-being.
5. Heal your relationships with your immediate family.
6. Live your life fully without the fear of death.
7. Allow your Spiritual Support Team to lead the way.
8. Be open to learning all lessons placed on your path.
9. Return your heart to a state of emotional and energetic wholeness.
10. Live your life in the present moment without regret of the past or fear of the future.
11. Love deeply, unconditionally and without the chains of emotional bondage.
12. Know (not just think, feel or believe) that you are in complete Oneness with All Being.

# PART III

# YESHUA CALLS FOR WORLD PEACE

**Yeshua:** *May HaShem bless each one of you on your path to becoming your Messiah Within. It must begin within each of you and then it will grow into a global energy called the Messiah Consciousness. When we live in the Messiah Consciousness then we will realize world peace. Therefore, how quickly this is achieved is really up to you. Dear Ones, I take my leave of you for now with the traditional prayer from the Shabbat Service:*

### Jewish Prayer for Peace

May we see the day when war and bloodshed cease
when a great peace will embrace the whole world.

Then nation shall not threaten nation
and humankind will not again know war.

For all who live on Earth shall realize
we have not come into being to hate or destroy.

We have come into being
to praise, to labour and to love.

Compassionate God, bless all the leaders of all nations
with the power of compassion.

Fulfill the promise conveyed in Scripture:
"I will bring peace to the land,
and you shall lie down and no one shall terrify you.

I will rid the land of vicious beasts
and it shall not be ravaged by war."

Let love and justice flow like a mighty stream.

Let peace fill the Earth as the waters fill the sea.

And let us say: Amen

**Robin:** Throughout my spiritual journey and in the course of my daily life, I am comforted and connected by reciting the Shema, the twice daily prayer of the Jewish people across the globe. The prayer is read as follows: *Sh'ma Yis'ra'eil Adonai Eloheinu Adonai echad.* Hear, O Israel, the Lord our God, the Lord is One. This has truly been the one prayer that has connected me to my Oneness with HaShem, Yeshua and my Spiritual Support Team. I interpret this simple but powerful prayer to mean that if the Lord our God is One and if we are made in the Divine image of HaShem, then we are One.

Yeshua says we need to join as One to create a new global energy of Messiah Consciousness. By taking to heart the words of the Shema, the Jewish people can bridge the gap between our ingrained cultural beliefs of separation and Yeshua's message of Oneness. May we be blessed to reach a global energy of Messiah Consciousness and ultimately an unprecedented era of world peace.

On behalf of all of the other Messengers of Divine Oneness on the planet today, working across and within our multi-cultural society, we wish you Godspeed in becoming your Messiah Within and your knowing of Oneness with All Being. I encourage you to connect with your Spiritual Support Team and to find a community that resonates with you and shares your values and beliefs. The energy of Oneness is very prevalent on the planet today, so you will not have to go far to find a community where you can join your energies together to share this important message.

I take my leave of you with one of my favorite stories from this period of my life.

One morning as I was crossing the bridge on Good Harbor Beach to watch a magnificent sunrise, a man passed me. The sunrise overlooking the island was majestic and the island was covered with a layer of fog all around the base. As I came off the bridge, he turned and walked back to me. He said, "Are we not the two luckiest people on the face of the Earth?" and I replied, "Indeed, we are." He then extended his hand and said to me, "My name is Bob and I am Oneness." I replied, "My name is Robin and I am Oneness, too."

# AFTERWORD
## GETTING TO KNOW YESHUA

Like a child in a candy store, I took this opportunity to ask Yeshua anything that was on my mind and what I thought you might like to understand from Yeshua's perspective. I came to realize that much of the conversation with Yeshua was not directly related to the steps to finding your Messiah Within but that they were critical to developing a relationship with him, to seeing him as a Messenger of The Divine and to honor the knowing that he was indeed in Oneness with All That Is. Many of the concepts presented below may make you uneasy, but I ask that you read them with an open heart and in the light within which we are so blessed to receive them.

### Yeshua—The Spiritual Icon

**Robin:** Yeshua, why do you think that you are such a controversial persona?

*Yeshua: That's a simple question to answer. Humanity sees in me the highest possible version of them. We spend our whole lives being in fear of what we desire the most and that is being in Oneness with God. The fear stems from the thought process that we can only achieve this "grand connection" when we die. But I was living proof that death is not a requirement for Oneness and, therefore, I represent achievement of the ultimate prize. What I have shared with you and many others on the planet over the past 2000 years is that true living is the recognition of your own divinity, not the day-to-day struggles of being human and accumulating stuff. Once you truly embrace this knowing, you begin to live in the flow of life and behold: life becomes easier. It takes great belief to see that by letting go of your desire to control your life and by surrendering to the universal flow of life, your life can be spent in joy and abundance.*

## Yeshua on God

**Robin:** Can you define God for us?

*Yeshua: Of course, God is you. But not just you, Robin, all of you. And not just humanity, but the animals, the trees, the planets—all of Creation. God is the collective energy of all life. It is so easy to think of God as a singular Being because we have placed God on a pedestal and, therefore, we have given God human traits. Especially those traits that are intended to create fear and have been used by mankind to control others through controlling their perception of the All-Mighty God. In Kabbalah, Jews use the term Ein Sof to describe God as infinite, without end, limitless. This is actually a very good description if we embrace the thinking that the essence or spark of God is present in all beings and, therefore, the sum of that energy is what we lovingly refer to as God.*

**Robin:** Why do our religious doctrines try to project God as angry or punishing?

*Yeshua: This is an interesting question because you can see that it contradicts what I am saying above. But if you look closely, it is not a contradiction. How can God be loving and kind one minute and angry and punishing the next? If God is the sum of the energy of all Beings, then doesn't it make sense that when life is peaceful on your planet or when the Earth has great storms that it could be the collective energy on the planet that is generating the outcomes that affect so many? Just like your thoughts, beliefs and actions create your personal reality, so it is the same with your planet. Notice how much quicker healing takes place on a devastated part of the planet when the whole world is praying for that area.*

## Yeshua—The Jewish Teacher

**Robin:** As a Jewish teacher, did you find that your teachings were not popular or contradicted the popular religious beliefs at the time?

*Yeshua: The desire to truly know God is timeless. In fact, that is why we gravitate towards religion in the first place. Well, perhaps many of us were made to go to religious services by our parents as children. But as adults we stick with it because it enables us to journey down the path towards knowing God. You were listening to a song just before," Shema" by Rita Glassman, and you were particularly taken with the words "Can you hear me, the One who has been calling you throughout the ages." HaShem (God) has been calling to all of mankind throughout the ages and the sound is even greater now as humanity begins to answer the call. For then it becomes an even louder voice—the Oneness of Mankind and God. If you are reading this and are feeling so close to this knowing or even totally lost on how to do this, listen for our collective voices. You will recognize us; we are the ones with the most open hearts and the greatest compassion even in times of perceived strife. In these times, when is seems that all is dark, those connected in Oneness with God will be like the lighthouse on the darkened seas. Follow the light and you will find us.*

**Robin:** Are you asking for everyone to follow the Torah?

*Yeshua: Can everyone become Jewish or can all Jews follow the Torah word-for-word? Of course not. God provided each of you with free will to make choices in your life. We understand that the hectic pace of your world does not allow for the luxury of an existence that is dedicated to the pursuit of religious study. What is required now is that mankind comes into a state of Oneness with God. That is why we are asking you to provide a blueprint for opening to— and reaching—a state of Oneness with the Divine. This will be the blueprint for others to find their own Messiah Within. We will define this blueprint with you throughout the book.*

**Robin:** Are we not contradicting the Torah by saying that the Messiah resides within?

*Yeshua: The most popular interpretation of the Messianic Age in the Torah is defined as a time yet to come and that a human will arrive that will bring the Jews into the Promised Land. I knew the Promised Land as not a physical location but as a state of being. My words have been written as "the Kingdom of God resides within." We are asking you to accept that the human who will bring you into the Promised Land is **yourself**. Every single person on the Earth plane is the Messiah; not just me or some mythical person yet to arrive, but **you**. Whenever you access your inner divinity you are reaching the Promised Land and you become the Messiah of your own life.*

**Robin:** Why have your teachings been lost to the Jews?

*Yeshua: I was quite amused with your words in your introduction that the Jewish people don't like to speak about me as either Yeshua ben Yosef or in my Christian persona, Jesus Christ. This is directly related to the Jewish people being wrongly accused of arranging for my death. After 2000 years of being wrongly accused of killing me, it is easy to understand your discomfort in accepting the teachings shared with me directly by HaShem. Let's go back 2000 years and look at my life as a Jewish teacher. I was deeply loved by the Jewish people in my lifetime, honored for my unique perspective and healing abilities. However, I was an extremely controversial presence in the world that I lived in. Because of my deep connection to the spiritual realm, I was able to heal individuals through their energetic field. These concepts are defined now through the school of medicine called Energy Medicine.*

*I'm sure you can all imagine how controversial I was; I talked about Oneness with God, I performed what were perceived as healing miracles using advanced energy healing techniques. My physical body was not a constraint in my life. It was a vessel used to contain Divine knowledge and healing energy to share with others. I spent most of my days in a state of Oneness and grace, therefore enabling me to access wisdom and tools far beyond the restrictions placed by the current religious political and healing systems of that time.*

*While I was extremely blessed, I was also a target for the political system. I was a threat, plain and simple. I could not be controlled by the Roman government because I was not afraid of them. They were afraid of me and what I represented. Therefore, I had to be stopped in their eyes. My teachings and my energy are very much a part of your world but with religious agendas dominating the original intentions.*

## Yeshua—As Jesus Christ

**Robin:** Can you share more about Christianity and its role in the delivery of your teachings?

*Yeshua: After my physical death, my students or disciples struggled for a mechanism by which to share my teachings. And, indeed, this was a struggle for them. For they knew the core of my teachings was that we did not need a religious structure to know God in Oneness. They also knew that the rigidity of the Torah protocols and the strict interpretation of the Torah language were not going to help humanity transcend into a state of grace and Oneness with the Divine. Therefore, they started a new movement, based on my teachings and without the formality of the Torah structure. And then, like any other structure, it required more formal governance. With the implementation of that governance, a desire for power arose and a desire to control the followers arose, resulting in a religious structure or system that is one of the largest and most controversial entities on the planet today.*

*The structure is so powerful in its utilization of fear as a tool to control its constituents—"do this or that or you will experience the wrath of God." There is no wrath of God—just unconditional love and support. It is from this platform that I make the same plea that I am making to the Jews—accept all mankind in Oneness. Place down your shields and your swords and embrace the gift that is mankind made in God's image.*

## Yeshua—On his greatest teaching, Unconditional Love

**Robin**: Whenever I read about your teachings, the words "unconditional love" are very prevalent. Can you share your thoughts on this concept with us?

*Yeshua: In its simplest form, unconditional love is the acceptance of another being without judgment.* Sounds rather simple, but what throws people off is the judgment piece. Humankind is in a perpetual state of judgment. "Why did someone say that? How will it affect me? Why do they look that way? Can I accept them with that flaw?" Do you recognize yourself in there? Most likely you all do. The bigger question is: can you learn to accept someone and/or their actions even if you don't agree with them? It is not a requirement to condone another's actions but it is possible to believe that they had an intention that in some way was in their highest and best good. Please know that you are loved unconditionally and from the spiritual realm there is absolutely no judgment.

## Yeshua—Reaching a Messiah Consciousness

**Robin:** How will each of the religious and spiritual paths find their Messiah Within?

*Yeshua: Ultimately we would like all humanity to establish a state of Oneness and each spiritual path or religion has been given the code to achieve this supreme outcome. For the Jews, God placed the code within the content of the Torah. When the Jewish people chose God, he knew that no matter what happened to the Jews, no matter what others tried to do to them, they would always guard the Torah with their lives and keep it sacred. Therefore, this code would remain safe until mankind was able to accept these teachings and understand their role in this sacred process. If the Jews can accept the rest of the world in Oneness, then HaShem can reveal the code hidden within the Torah to bring Heaven to Earth to have God fully reside on the Earth plane.*

*This code is not unique to the Jews; this is simply the particular code that the Jews will relate to. Many, many cultures are working on this now, too, but in this book I am focusing attention on my fellow Jews. It is God's desire that the Jews be part of this global awakening. However, this cannot occur if the Jewish people still harbor a stubborn and persistent persecution complex. The Divine is ready to share the code hidden in the Torah for the Jewish people to reach a state of spiritual Oneness with all Jews and then with all other souls on the planet—and with HaShem.*

**Robin:** Why have the Jews not found the code up to now?

*Yeshua: Up to now, the Torah has been viewed as a manual for living the perfect Jewish life. The Jews have used it as a set of directions and prescriptions for honoring God in all of His magnificence in our daily rituals. Included in the rituals are ways to "reach up to Heaven to find God and bring God down to Earth". Hidden in the Torah is the* code that will enable the Jews to accept that God is not "out there" and does not need any type of mechanism to go back and forth to Heaven, but that God resides within each of us.

We are asking for the Jews to look at the Torah with a new eye, one that shows how to live in Oneness with God on the Earth plane. Each person must learn to honor his or her body and heart center as the new home of God. To know that their own inner divinity is the Promised Land, that their heart becomes fully open to being the Divine temple for God to reside in, that God is here now in every one of us.

**Robin:** How will the code be cracked?

*Yeshua: We have shared with you the person who will crack the code. He has been given his directive and now it is up to him to live his life's work. For privacy reasons, we will not share his name with the readers but we are confident that he is prepared for this task and will rise to the occasion. Be his friend and support his efforts. We have placed you in close proximity so that you can work together on this. Help him to create sacred space that brings in all support from the spiritual realm. I am available to both of you as often as you need me.*

## Yeshua—On Mass Genocide

**Robin:** Can you explain the Holocaust and other mass genocides on the planet?

*Yeshua: Throughout the ages, some groups have attempted to dominate mankind. In many cases, they have succeeded and caused great grief and loss of life. There are many facets to these unfortunate times. The first one to reiterate is that we each come into this lifetime with a role to play and a destiny to fulfill. This is contracted at the soul level prior to entering your human body. However, as established with our first humans, we were given what is called "Free Will." Free will is the opportunity to influence our destiny by making personal decisions on how to act in situations to influence how they are going to be played out.*

*We also previously talked about a persecution complex that can hold very strong karmic energy amongst a group or tribe of people. When this persecution complex is greater in energy than the Free Will of the people, the more dominant group is able to more easily control the will of the persecuted. Of course, powerful weapons help, but it is the expectation of a persecutory outcome based on generational fears that will enable the more dominant to be successful in achieving what they may convince even themselves is a necessary evil.*

*Do atrocities such as these exist to teach important lessons to mankind, and should we never forget them? Yes, but the lessons to be learned are for both the persecutors and for the persecuted. We must all learn to accept each other without judgment and see each other in Oneness. But until that happens we leave ourselves vulnerable to fulfill a destiny that may be more one of tribal energy versus one of our own personal destiny, which we can more easily influence with our gift of free will.*

## Yeshua—On Near-Death Experiences

**Robin:** Can you share with us your perspective on near-death experiences? Why do some people die and then come back to life?

*Yeshua: Yes, this is a topic that many of you are reluctant to believe in. Many near-death experiences happen at the time of great harm or stress to the physical body. This physical harm does not always correspond to the time that the soul agreed to leave the planet. Therefore, part of the earthly experience becomes learning to live and survive the great pain, hurt or stress on the physical body and the subsequent stress on the mental, emotional and spiritual bodies. It may not sound fair but it was the agreement that was made. At times like this, the body may give out and the soul makes its way into the Light, but we have to request that the soul return to physicality to complete its original purpose for incarnating during that lifetime.*

*Other times, perhaps during attempted suicides, we are able to reason with the soul and have it return to the Earth plane and its physical vessel to complete its incarnation. And yet at other times, we are able to share with individual souls their next level gifts and that is why you see so many individuals who have had near-death experiences become more open to their spiritual gifts. And the last example is when we can extend someone's incarnation to fulfill a desire or mission. Your father was a good example of this. Do you want to share his story?*

**Robin:** When my father, George was fifty years old, he had a triple by-pass heart surgery. During the surgery, they could not bring him back off the by-pass heart machine. It was pretty touch and go for a while. My dad said that during that time, he was in the Light and he asked for a gift of *Chai* (which is Hebrew for the gift of another eighteen years, or a Lifetime, as defined in Judaism). He wanted to see his children marry and meet his first round of grandchildren. He truly knew that he would pass eighteen years close to his first surgery and would remind me of that often. I was too spiritually naïve to believe him and besides the medical opportunities afforded him did not support that.

In the upcoming 14 years, he would have another triple heart by-pass surgery and finally a heart transplant. He was given the heart of a young man and the doctors said that the longer he did not reject the new heart the better his chances of living. So, after the transplant, he would say to me, "I only have 4 years" and the next year only 3, and the year after that only 2. And then the last year, his new heart began to fail which, in turn, meant his other vital organs began to fail. But he would look at me and say, "I told you that I only had *Chai* to live." He died within three months of the eighteenth anniversary of his first surgery.

Many of you might think that he gave himself a self-fulfilling prophecy. On one hand I agree with you—it was a self-fulfilling prophecy because it was an agreement he had with the Divine. On the other hand, he lived his life in a manner that gave him the most enjoyment because he knew his time was limited. The irony is that this is the same for all of us—our time is also limited in our physical bodies. We just don't know if we have 18 days, 18 years or 88 years. I wish that I could have "believed" him at the time, but I was not ready on my spiritual path to understand this concept. I can say that we had a wonderful eighteen years and for that I am eternally grateful.

## Yeshua—The Children

**Robin**: Yeshua, can you talk about the extraordinary children who have graced our planet?

*Yeshua: For the past 30 years, we have been bringing in smaller generations of children with exceptional spiritual gifts. In the mainstream world, you have labeled them as having Down syndrome, ADHD and Autism. These amazing children have been sent into this world to teach you how to love unconditionally and to have greater tolerance and patience. We are not happy to see them medicated in order to have them conform to your standardized schools or programs.*

*As you have seen with the first round of special children, the Down syndrome children, they make wonderful contributions to their families and workplace, bringing joy to everyone who knows them. For the special children labeled ADHD, they have exceptional intellect and are just plain bored with your limited learning systems. Their behavior is borne out of frustration, not out of being intrinsically "bad." And, last but not least, the beautiful Autistic children . . . they are made from Light and have no doubt whatsoever that they are communicating with each other. As the other humans on the planet increase their own light, the communication will become more enhanced. For parents of these beautiful souls, we encourage you to bring more light into your own physical and energetic bodies so that you can relate more fully to these children. We also encourage you to allow Autistic children to gather together in groups to send light out onto the planet. They are tremendous healers and if their energy is harnessed together, the impact will be powerful.*

*During this same 30-year period, we have been bringing in the next round of leaders for your world. They have come in the forms labeled as Indigo, Rainbow, Crystal and the New children. Many of the early arrivers were given the label ADHD but, we promise you, these children are here to lead humanity into our next wave of evolution. The New children being born today are extremely precious. They are coming with no karmic history; in essence they are pure souls. Watch for these special babies and love them unconditionally, but most of all, keep them brave and not fearful. If we can keep them brave, they will truly bring Heaven to Earth for all of the inhabitants and including Mother Earth. It is important to allow them to be their Authentic Selves as well, so that they may fulfill their important destinies on the Earth plane.*

## Yeshua—On World Peace

**Robin:** If we have never had an unprecedented era of world peace on our planet, how will the children described above know how to bring about this golden age?

*Yeshua: This question has many answers so let's begin. First of all, as described above, all of the children born in the past 30 years have come into their lives with a very clear understanding of what their paths are. Many of them are just waiting to grow up to accomplish what they came here to do. Do you remember meeting one of the new children in your holistic healing center? Do you want to share that story?*

**Robin:** Of course, I was sitting in the waiting room talking to a client and I see this baby travel chair on the floor. The baby was straining its neck and back to look out of the seat at me. He was the most beautiful baby—he looked like a Buddha in a baby body. I got up out of my chair and I went over to his seat. When I looked in the seat, I exclaimed, "Oh my goodness, it's one of the New children!" I am not quite sure how I knew this but I knew it. Within the next few minutes, one of our Spiritual Channels came out of a healing room and I said, "Check out this beautiful baby". She looked in the seat and said, "That's not a baby, that's a man." Yeshua, his energy was extraordinary. Thank goodness, he has parents that will honor these qualities in him. What can we share with the parents of these children to help them first recognize and then honor the gifts that the children have?

*Yeshua: While it is important to honor the gifts of the youngest children that we call the New children, it is important to know that this is not a handful of children but we are referring to an entire generation of children that have been born during this time of great shift in consciousness that began in the late 1980's. Therefore, how do we raise an entire generation of children to be each a world leader in their own right? The answer is very simple, we raise these children as we have always raised our children, with love, compassion, solid education, personal pride and an appreciation for their fellow man and all inhabitants of the Earth. We teach them that each person on the Earth is responsible for the Earth and all inhabitants and most of all they are responsible for themselves and therefore, they must make a contribution to the greater good. This contribution does not require that they become the President of the Free World but that they become a citizen of the Earth. A globally conscious person who is passionate about their fellow man and all inhabitants of the Earth.*

*For you see, world peace begins within each of you. For too long, we have viewed world peace as something outside of ourselves. Here is a good example; you walk into a room and there are five people in the room. All five of them are arguing over something. Think about how you feel now—frustrated, nervous and not happy to be there.*

*What if you walked in the room and the five people were laughing, hugging each other and talking about how much they love their lives; how would you feel then? Of course, you would come into the room smiling and perhaps anxious to add your story to the mix of story being shared and grab a hug or two!*

*In the second scenario, we could easily say that the five people were exemplifying world peace. See how easy that could be to become world peace as a single person. This is the type of day to day living that we must create for the children of the Earth. This will require a review of our parenting, education and entertainment systems that are currently in place. How can you expect your children to participate in this movement towards world peace, when they are subjected to an entertainment industry that sells violence? You need to be the watch keepers of these sacred souls. Honor them and you will fulfill your destiny as well.*

**Robin:** Around the first time that I heard your message, "As the Chosen People, the Jews can choose World Peace", I read an article with an interesting message that was channeled by another person on the planet. The message was that world peace will truly come to be with the Abrahamic Religions (or the Jews, Christians and the Muslims) when they re-build the temple in Jerusalem together. The channeled message also said that this may not take place in my lifetime. However, I have recently received a request in a channeled message from King Solomon that it is time to re-build the temple in Jerusalem. Could you provide me with your insight on this extraordinary message?

*Yeshua: King Solomon built the first ancient temple in Jerusalem known as the First Temple on the Temple Mount. This was a temple of peace as it was built during a time of peace. There are many interesting aspects to this message that you received and it would be best to let King Solomon share directly with you what he has in mind. This will be the topic of your next book.*

*In this book, King Solomon will address finding the hidden temple within your heart (the next logical step after finding your Messiah Within) and then he will move on to physically rebuilding the Temple in Jerusalem. King Solomon will address the technology that he used to build the temple or the technology used to build all of the great ancient sites that existed on the planet. The technology King Solomon used was ancient and advanced at the same time. His teachings will enable the children of the Earth to create new sources of energy for our planet. A physical structure or Temple will once again be built in Jerusalem by the children of all the Abrahamic religions.*

*Yes, they are children now but not forever. The children today are carrying the higher energy frequencies to re-instate this technology on the planet. The technologies revealed will provide clean, renewable energy sources required for the long-term survival of our planet. What your readers will come to know if that the ancient technologies are not of this planet and finally, the veil will be lifted from humanity to take its rightful place in the planetary alliance.*

**Robin:** How exciting! I look forward to writing this book as all of the topics you listed are of great interest to me. Or perhaps they became of great interest to me because I was being prepared to write this second book. To be the channel for King Solomon for this next book is a great honor—thank you.

## Yeshua—Views on Modern Spirituality

**Robin:** I have studied with a variety of teachers who either confirm or oppose the concepts of Past Lives and the carrying our eternal blueprint in our DNA. Can you elaborate on this?

*Yeshua: Each soul is part of a network of energy called All Being. Included in All Being are beings of multiple dimensions, shapes, sizes and DNA make-ups. For the "Human" Being, you have been blessed to be able to carry forward both past and current life experiences as stored memories in your DNA structure. You are able to review or recall these memories in your current lifetime. If you are willing to take this path of understanding and release past traumatic experiences, then you will grow significantly on your path.*

**Robin:** Why do we have such a difficult time recognizing the Divine presence in ourselves and others?

*Yeshua: Let's step back a moment and talk about the human experience. The premise from which most spiritual teachers today are working is that: we are energetic beings (sparks from All Being) having a human experience (thus the term human being). Therefore, when your soul enters your body in the womb, your body becomes hardwired with its spiritual guidance. For many, many generations, this connection diminished as you became more greatly influenced by the emotions and teachings of the important human beings in your life (parents, teachers, siblings, and friends). Especially in the Western World, your spiritual connection is downplayed tremendously. In the Eastern World, there is a far greater emphasis placed on the spiritual self.*

**Robin:** Why have so many spiritual teachers come to this planet at this exact moment in time?

*Yeshua: Because we are now in a time of great shift on the planet. Both humanity and Mother Earth and her inhabitants are raising their consciousness and vibration all at once. This is creating a great deal of turmoil and fear in many humans at this time. In addition, there is a perceived sense of lack or scarcity because life as you knew it is now ending.*

*The world is not coming to an end, as many believe, but your reliance on money and personal assets as an indicator of your self-*

*worth is now ending. In the near future, your self-worth will be measured by the number of people whom you love unconditionally, by the service that you provide to others and by how you live in unity with all inhabitants of, and including, Mother Earth.*

**Robin:** Many spiritual teachers have said that we are bringing Heaven to Earth. Can you explain this idea?

**Yeshua:** *This time period on the Earth has been described as the time of Ascension. It seems like we are reaching towards the heavens. That is actually correct—because you are each reaching towards the Heaven that resides within you. The process of finding your Messiah Within is the process of Ascension. Therefore, the process of Ascension is the path to finding your inner divinity and the knowing that God resides right here on the Earth plane in each one of you.*

*Even if we speak using the popular jargon of "transitioning from our current 3rd dimensional (Homo Sapien) bodies to our 5th dimensional (Homo Luminous) bodies," we are still talking about staying put right here on the Earth plane. Life will just be more connected to one and all.*

**Robin:** What do you mean by accessing your own inner divinity?

*Yeshua: Ah, we love this question, because here is where we get to make it simpler for you. Your inner divinity is whatever ever brings you the most joy in your life. Up to now, you might have been thinking, "Do I have to have some great mystical experience or spiritual awakening to find my Messiah Within?" No, you don't. You can find this in the joys of living your everyday life. You can find this whenever you have experienced unconditional love or are connected in joy to another person, animal, plant or the Earth herself. The possibilities are endless.*

*We made your process, Robin, a bit more complicated because you needed to experience the mystical moments in order to wake up faster and be the conduit for these teachings. You volunteered for this job on your soul level long before you even arrived on the planet in this physical form. Many of your peers did as well, and you are all teaching these concepts in what might be perceived as everyday jobs, in your relationships with each other and in your relationship with the Earth.*

**Robin:** Why can some people connect to the spiritual realm and others cannot? I am talking about Spiritual Messengers.

*Yeshua: Everyone, and I mean everyone, can connect to the spiritual realm; many just choose not to. Even when you sit in a house of worship, or watch a beautiful sunset or hug a child, the unconditional love that you feel is the connection to the spiritual realm. Professionals who share information with others from the spiritual realm are just much more comfortable with the process and they have recognized that they have a gift to do this and are willing to share their gift. In every profession there are dishonest people, and these professions have their fair share. When reaching out to your earthly Spiritual Support Team, we ask you to honor your intuition about a person first and to get references if needed. Even if you were to use only mainstream, credentialed professionals like a rabbi, minister or therapist, we are confident you would follow the same process. That is the best way to know if any Messenger is right for you.*

**Robin:** If everyone knows their spiritual path on an intuitive level, why are they all not on it?

*Yeshua: Because for now, it takes a significant effort to clear away the debris from our current and past lives and to step away from the noise and distractions of your planet to a place of inner quiet. It would mean turning off all your electronic equipment so that you could listen to your heart. Notice that we said heart and not mind. That is because the heart is your connection to the Divine; the mind enables you to have sacred inquiry but the heart is the key. The greater we can uncover, clear and heal our heart on an energetic basis, the faster mankind can find their Messiahs Within.*

*This is truly not a race, but the Divine can guarantee that there is a lovely prize for everyone at the finish line. While it took you ten years to follow the path, we are confident that with the pace of consciousness-raising on the planet today, it will happen even faster for others.*

## Yeshua—His Greatest Desire

**Robin:** What is your greatest desire for mankind?

*Yeshua: My greatest desire for mankind is twofold. The first is to see me for who I truly was. I was neither Yeshua ben Yosef or Jesus Christ, but I was a Messenger for the Divine. I incarnated on this Earth to provide you all with the information that could lead mankind into a state of unprecedented peace and compassion for each other and the other inhabitants of the Earth. And yet, mankind took my teachings of unconditional love and Oneness and used them to create fear and to justify unspeakable acts against each other.*

*My second greatest desire is for all of mankind to accept my teachings in their truest essence and to honor these teachings for every man, woman and child on the planet. When we can reach a state of Oneness with each other, the healing of the animals and the planet will fall naturally into place. Therefore, it is truly up to each one of you to create Heaven on Earth. Are you up to the task?*

**Robin:** Thank you, Yeshua. Shalom for now!

# ABOUT THE AUTHOR

Robin Clare is the co-founder of two spiritual organizations: Enlightened Professionals, for the advancement of the careers of spiritual and holistic professionals, and The ATMA Center, where spiritual seekers can associate with other like-minded individuals in a variety of spiritual and holistic pursuits. Over a ten-year period, Robin has been on a journey of self-discovery to allow her life's purpose to fully manifest in service to others. As a spiritual businessperson, teacher, life coach, and channeler, Robin has had the privilege to live a life grounded in spiritual concepts. *Messiah Within* represents the culmination of her journey of deep reflection and communication with her Spiritual Support Team—on this Earth and beyond. Through the pursuit of her spiritual path, Robin discovered her true life purpose … and her own Messiah Within. Robin offers her insights gathered along that journey, so that you may do the same. Robin lives in Connecticut with her family.